The UK Economy 2007-2017

Nick Fyfe
Head of Economics, Dulwich College

Andrew Threadgould
Staff Tutor, Dulwich College

informe

Contents

Chapter 1
GDP: Boom, Bust and Recovery

Introduction

The story of UK GDP growth between 2007 and 2017 is complex. The 'NICE' decade of Non-Inflationary Continuous Expansion ended with the credit crisis of 2007 and was followed by the recession of 2008-09. In the years since, the UK economy has returned to growth with output rising and unemployment falling alongside low inflation, but new threats to stability and prosperity are emerging.

● Knowledge: **Economic growth**

Economic growth – the increase in the productive capacity in an economy – is a fundamental measure of macroeconomic performance. The trend rate of economic growth for the UK economy has been assumed for several years to be between 2.5% and 2.75% per year. This implies that the total output of the economy, if all factors of production (land, labour, capital, enterprise) were fully utilised, would grow by this percentage each year.

However measuring productive capacity is very difficult, and thus economists focus on the more accessible measure of economic growth as the percentage change in Gross Domestic Product (GDP). GDP measures actual output: the total value of output in the whole economy over a given period of time.

● Application: **A brief history of UK growth**

Figure 1.1: UK real GDP growth

Source: HM Treasury

As Figure 1.1 shows, the actual growth rate of the UK economy has fluctuated significantly from year to year.

A **recession** occurs where real GDP growth is negative for at least two consecutive quarters. Over the period shown in Figure 1.1 the UK economy experienced two recessions: in the early 1990s and in 2008-09. In addition, the UK economy was initially believed to have re-entered recession in late 2011 and early 2012 but later revisions of the data showed this was narrowly avoided. A **boom** is a period during which real GDP rises at a faster rate than assumed growth in productive capacity. The long boom of 1997-2007 can clearly be seen in Figure 1.1.

Recovery, or upturn, often marks the period between the end of a recession and the beginning of a boom. During this stage of the economic cycle, real GDP is positive, rising, but still below the long-run growth rate. On the other hand, a slowdown or downturn occurs when real GDP growth is positive but falling and is below the long-run growth rate.

> ### Question
>
> 1. Using Figure 1.1, give examples of each of the following: boom, slowdown, recession, recovery.

Macroeconomic policies tend to focus on creating stable and sustainable economic growth. **Supply-side policies** aim to increase the long-run average, or trend level of growth which shows increases in productive capacity. This will be explored in greater detail in Chapter 6 when we examine productivity and competitiveness in greater detail. **Demand-management policies** such as fiscal and monetary measures are used to control actual GDP and take a shorter-term approach to macroeconomic stability. These policies are explored in greater depth in Chapters 9 and 10 respectively.

When investigating the story of the UK in recent years, economic growth is a key indicator of the health and potential of the UK macroeconomy.

● ● Application and Analysis: **Components of UK GDP**

GDP measures the total value of output, expenditure and incomes across the economy over a given period of time. Macroeconomists break down GDP into four key areas:

Consumption (C)   Spending by households on consumer goods e.g. food, holidays, clothes

Investment (I)   Spending by firms on capital goods e.g. machinery, vehicles, plant

Government Spending (G) Spending by the public sector e.g. infrastructure, public sector wages, NHS costs

Net Exports (X-M)   Spending by foreigners on UK goods minus spending by the UK on foreign goods

Figure 1.2: UK GDP by component

Source: HM Treasury

Figure 1.2 shows the importance of consumer spending for the UK economy over the period shown. The effect of the recession in 2008-09 can be seen on both consumption and investment, along with the fall in net exports resulting from recession in the UK's main trading partners.

Figure 1.3: Economic growth in the UK by component

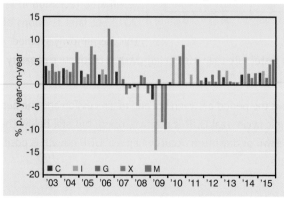

Source: HM Treasury

Figure 1.3 shows how each of these components changed over the same period.

● Analysis: **Explaining fluctuations in real GDP growth**

Figure 1.4: UK business confidence in the service and manufacturing sector

Source: HM Treasury

Figure 1.5: UK consumer confidence

Source: HM Treasury

1991-1997: Recession and export-led growth

The UK experienced recession in the early 1990s. Stock markets crashed in 1987 in the USA and across Europe. The UK economy continued to grow until 1990 but as oil prices were pushed higher by the Gulf War, both consumer price inflation and the base rate reached double figures. Falling real incomes and the negative wealth effect from a struggling housing market pushed the UK into its deepest recession since the Second World War. In September 1992 the domestic currency, sterling, was forced out of the Exchange Rate Mechanism, which was the system used to ensure national currencies converged in preparation for the creation of the single European currency, the euro.

The period 1992-97 saw recovery from recession. The weaker value of sterling helped to boost exports, particularly to other European countries, and there was growth in the service sector and the UK economy began to emerge as a modern, service-based consumer economy.

Spending by households on consumer goods such as clothes is the most important element of UK GDP.

Figure 1.6: UK base rate of interest

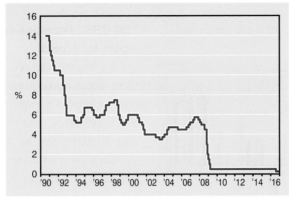

Source: Bank of England

Figure 1.7: UK unemployment

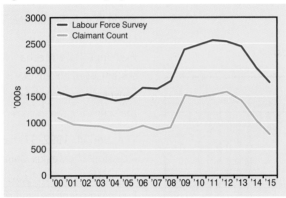

Source: HM Treasury

Figure 1.8: Long-term and youth unemployment in the UK

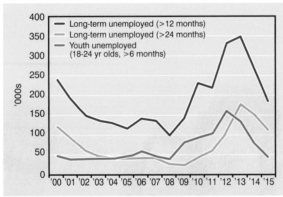

Source: HM Treasury

Figure 1.9: UK inflation, Consumer Price Index

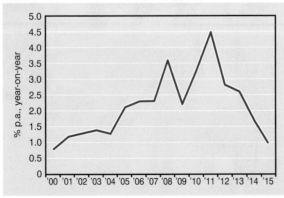

Source: HM Treasury

1997-2000: Early days of New Labour

With a New Labour government in place with an emphasis on growth and economic stability, the UK economy began a period of significant expansion. The control of monetary policy and the setting of interest rates was handed to the newly-independent Bank of England and the intention of significant public sector investment in education and healthcare was clear.

The 'feel good factor' returned to the UK economy:

● interest rates fell through 1998 and 1999 (from 7.25% in May 1998 to 5% by June 1999; figures for 1990-2016 are shown on Figure 1.6).

● unemployment continued to fall, in particular long-term and youth unemployment.

● low and falling inflationary pressure.

● the housing market experienced its strongest growth since the early 1990s, increasing household wealth through positive equity for homeowners (Figure 1.10).

● strong stock market performance, increasing household wealth for shareholders (Figure 1.11).

During the years 1997-2000 the housing market experienced its strongest growth since the early 1990s.

Figure 1.10: UK housing market indicators

Source: HM Treasury

Figure 1.11: FTSE All Share Index, annual average

Source: HM Treasury

Figure 1.12: NASDAQ Composite Index, annual average

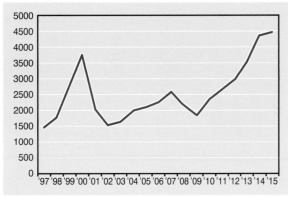

Source: HM Treasury

Figure 1.13: Annual change in selected stock market indices

Source: HM Treasury

2000-2003: Turbulent times

By the turn of the millennium, it was clear the 'mini-boom' of 1997-2000 was coming to an end. The FTSE index increased by less than 5% over 2000 compared to double-digit growth in 1996-99 (see Figure 1.11). Even before the terrorist attacks in New York in September 2001, the US economy had faltered as the dot-com boom (and associated economic expansion created by the growth of new technology spending and investment) came to an end.

On March 10, 2000 the NASDAQ (the second-largest stock exchange in the USA, which pioneered online trading and was the exchange of choice for the new technology firms associated with the internet boom of 1995-2000) Composite index reached its peak of 5,132.52. Figure 1.12 shows the *average* annual values of this index between 1997 and 2015.

Over the course of 2001, the NASDAQ lost almost half of its value, with significant losses also recorded on the Dow Jones and FTSE indices (Figure 1.13).

These problems in the US economy were compounded by the tragic events in New York on the 9th September 2001, and the economic impact in the UK was one of shaken confidence and fears for future growth. The saving ratio for UK households, which had fallen steadily since the early 1990s recorded a small increase in 2001 (see Figure 1.14), and house price growth dipped in 2000 and 2001, albeit still increasing above the rate of inflation (housing market transactions also continued to rise as shown in Figure 1.15).

Figure 1.14: UK saving ratio

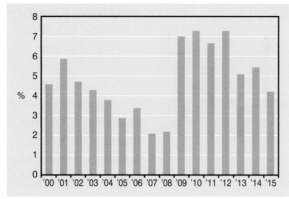

Source: HM Treasury

Figure 1.15: UK housing market inflation

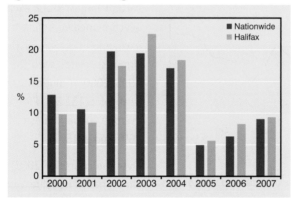

Source: HM Treasury

Figure 1.16: UK budget position at constant 2010-11 prices

Source: HM Treasury

Figure 1.17: UK economic data

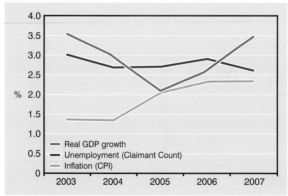

Source: HM Treasury

The period 2000 to 2003 also marked a shift towards greater fiscal injection into the economy. The New Labour government elected in 1997 had stuck to Conservative spending plans for its first two years in office, but after a second election victory in May 2001 the budget surpluses built up in the years 1998-2001 (Figure 1.16) and were viewed by Chancellor Gordon Brown as being available to fund significant public sector investment.

2003-2007: Steady, stable growth

The period begins with house price inflation of over 20% according to the Halifax index as shown in Figure 1.15. The second half of 'the NICE decade' (a period of Non-Inflationary Continuous Expansion) of 1997-2007 was a period of recovering economic growth after the problems of 2000-01.

Real GDP growth began and ended this period above its trend rate of 2.5%, unemployment fell and inflation was under control. This stability allowed business and consumer confidence to recover in the UK; nonetheless, the current account position moved into a large deficit, most significantly as the imports of goods grew far more quickly than exports, as shown in Figure 1.18.

The base rate was increased steadily from 3.50% in July 2003 to 5.75% in July 2007 (see Figure 1.6). Interest rates – a flagship independent policy of the New Labour government – played a significant role in the story of the UK economy at that time; this is discussed in greater detail in Chapter 9. Interest rate changes influence the wider economy by influencing the consumer and business decision on whether to spend or save; they also directly influence the value of the domestic currency in foreign exchange markets through effects on the patterns of global saving and investment. Higher interest rates put upward pressure on the value of sterling, making exports more expensive and imports cheaper. However, consumer spending remained strong due to a structural movement towards lower saving across the economy. Despite higher consumption and

Figure 1.18: UK current account position

Source: HM Treasury

Figure 1.19: UK interest rate (LIBOR) differential with interest rates in Germany and USA (UK minus foreign rate)

Source: HM Treasury

the added injection of a heavy public sector investment programme, inflation remained low, suppressed by falling import prices and the powerful force of globalisation. Thus UK interest rates were a dangerous combination of *historically low* but nevertheless *relatively high* compared with interest rates elsewhere. Figure 1.6 showed earlier in this chapter how the base rate was significantly higher in the early 1990s than a decade later. Figure 1.19 compares UK interest rates with those of Germany and the USA during the NICE decade. The differential in the UK interest rate with Germany was 1.5% or more in all but three years, and of the same size as compared with the USA in all but five years.

Question

2. Using the ideas from this chapter so far, identify the factors which might contribute to strong economic growth in an economy.

2007-2017: Recession, recovery, relapse?

Despite the false alarms of 2000-01, UK economic growth and related consumer indicators (most notably the housing market and stock exchange) recovered strongly up to the summer of 2007, when it became obvious that the longest period of positive economic growth since World War Two was coming to an end. The US housing market had peaked in early 2006, fuelled in part by the subprime lending market where banks were willing to issue mortgages to householders previously deemed too risky to lend to. As borrowers defaulted on loans, banks were forced to absorb these losses and in many cases required assistance from national governments to remain in business.

Figure 1.20: UK GDP – the recession of 2008-09

Source: HM Treasury

Business and consumer confidence collapsed (see Figures 1.4 and 1.5) and public sector finances, already under strain as unemployment began to rise, had to be diverted to support financial institutions and avert a total collapse in the banking sector.

After 63 quarters of positive economic growth the UK economy entered recession, recording negative growth in the second quarter of 2008 of -1.3%. Growth remained negative until the third quarter of 2009 (see Figure 1.20).

Analysis: **Causes of the UK recession, 2008-2009**

The economic conditions of 2007-09 are regarded by some economists as a 'perfect storm': a combination of factors which combined to drive the economy into recession. These factors are:

- a financial crisis which increased the costs of borrowing for firms and households as banks feared collapse due to their exposure to bad debts.

- a subsequent tightening of access to finance for both households and firms.

- falling house prices (especially in the USA), exposing mortgage lenders to serious losses and reducing consumer confidence and household wealth.

- significant losses on stock markets.

- high levels of household debt due to cheap, easy finance and a falling saving ratio in the NICE decade.

- rising oil prices (an increase from $55 to $147 per barrel between early 2007 and July 2008).

As aggregate demand (total spending in the economy; the sum of consumption, investment, government expenditure and net exports) fell, further problems were created.

Analysis: **Impacts of the UK recession, 2008-2009**

The credit crisis and consequent 'Great Recession' at the end of the 2000s created a sharper contraction in economic activity in the UK than any time since the second world war, with output falling more than at the beginning of the 1990s.

- rising joblessness, particularly for long-term and youth unemployment

- fewer job vacancies as firms avoided recruitment due to uncertainty about the future.

- falling living standards as average earnings fell (impact of higher unemployment bringing average earnings down, as well as pay freezes and below-inflation pay awards for those people still in work).

- higher demand for higher education places as school-leavers (and graduates pursuing postgraduate courses) sought to remain in education.

- a fall in inflation on the RPI measure (Figure 1.21); the differences between CPI and RPI and therefore the explanation for the significant disparity between these measures in 2009 are discussed in Chapter 8.

- a depreciation in sterling (see Chapter 5).

- pressure on the government's budget position, as tax revenues fell (due to downward pressure on incomes, spending and wealth) and spending increased (due to the automatic stabiliser of more unemployment benefit claimants).

Figure 1.21: RPI and CPI in UK

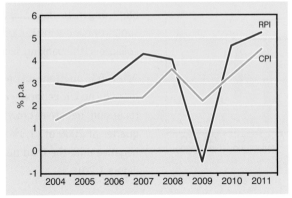

Source: HM Treasury

● Analysis: **Anti-recession policies**

The key policy instruments available to governments to control the level of aggregate demand in the economy are monetary and fiscal measures.

Monetary policy (This is discussed in detail in Chapter 9):

● drastic cuts in the base rate of interest (see Figure 1.6) culminating in a historically unprecedented base rate of 0.50% from March 2009, and 0.25% from August 2016.

● a programme of quantitative easing beginning in March 2009: the purchase of government debt by the Bank of England (by February 2012, the Bank had authorised purchases of up to £375bn).

● acceptance of a fall in the value of sterling, reducing the price of UK goods in international markets and stimulating export performance.

Fiscal policy (This is discussed in detail in Chapter 10):

● cuts in tax rates, such as the temporary reduction in VAT from 17.5% to 15% in December 2008.

● increases in other taxes, such as the introduction of a top rate of income tax of 50% on earnings over £150,000 per annum and a reduction of tax relief on pensions for high earners.

● higher government spending on initiatives such as an extra £1.7bn on the job centre network, to support job seekers, and to help businesses during difficult trading conditions.

● the scope for fiscal expansion has been limited due to the government's focus on closing the budget deficit ('austerity' policies) rather than to stimulate GDP growth to trigger automatic stabilisers.

> ### Question
>
> 3. Which policies are likely to be most effective in reducing the severity of a recession?

● Evaluation: **The impact of austerity**

Figure 1.22: UK GDP, quarter-on-quarter growth (%)

Source: HM Treasury

Figure 1.22 shows the quarterly growth data for the UK economy.

UK GDP returned to its pre-crisis level in Q2 of 2014 as the economy grew at an annualised rate of 3.1%. Relevant economic indicators will be explored in the chapters ahead, but even with the shock result of the EU referendum result and arising uncertainty of the future trading position with the EU, the economy has continued to record positive quarterly growth into 2017.

There are several arguments explaining the story of GDP growth since 2009, including:

● Austerity measures have boosted confidence and innovation in the private sector of the economy, creating a 'crowding-in' dynamic and sustainable job creation and output.

● Austerity has slowed down the recovery: fiscal stimulus, rather than fiscal contraction, would have returned the economy to growth more quickly, reducing unemployment (and associated benefits) and generating tax revenue earlier.

- 'Austerity' is a myth: the Coalition government made pledges to cut the size of the government and national debt, but in reality the economy remained reliant on government spending to maintain recovery. Phillip Hammond, the new Chancellor under Theresa May, announced a programme of infrastructure spending in the Autumn Statement in November 2016 which looks surprisingly 'Keynesian' in its fiscal stance!

- Recovery continues to look unbalanced (regionally, and in terms of income levels) and dependent on cheap credit, fuelling another consumption and housing boom despite increasing levels of job insecurity in some sectors and uncertainty regarding the UK's trading relationship with the EU.

Question

4. Has austerity helped or hindered economic recovery in the UK?

The result of the referendum in June 2016 on whether the UK should remain in the European Union will be an important factor determining the future level and pattern of growth in the years ahead. The shape and timing of 'Brexit' will be discussed throughout this book. The shape and timing of 'Brexit' will be discussed throughout this book; it is likely to have a more significant influence on both the level and pattern of economic growth than any other event in recent economic history.

● Evaluation: Gain and pain in a recession

'Winners' in a recession	'Losers' in a recession
Firms	
● Lower wage inflation	● Lower demand, especially for luxury goods
● Larger pool of available workers, some of whom may be highly skilled and desperate to work	● Negative equity as land and property prices decline
● Higher demand for inferior goods as consumers switch down to less expensive options	● Possible bankruptcy
● Higher domestic demand if currency depreciates, as imports become more expensive	
Households	
● Lower borrowing costs and mortgage repayments as base rate is cut	● Falling real income levels (especially if inflation remains relatively high)
● Lower income tax rates if government uses fiscal policy to stimulate the economy	● More expensive imports and foreign holidays due to weaker currency
● Cheaper goods and services as firms compete more aggressively for business	● Threat of unemployment and resulting poverty and hardship

Extension Question

5. What might be the likely effects of 'Brexit' on the UK economy in the years ahead?

Chapter 2

Consumer Spending, Saving and Credit

In this chapter we consider in detail how household expenditure in the UK has moved and discuss the factors which explain differences in the growth rate of this spending.

● Knowledge: **Consumption, saving, credit and income**

The concepts of consumer spending, saving and credit are intrinsically linked. **Consumer spending**, also known as **consumption**, is spending by households on goods and services. The most obvious determinant of the consumption level in an economy is **income**. However, households can fund spending from income in different time periods.

- **Past income** – households can draw on **savings** (income previously earned and not consumed) to fund consumption now.

- **Current income** – the most obvious source of funds for consumer spending, but most households will usually try to save some of their income to plan for the future or prepare for contingencies.

- **Future income** – effectively, households can spend future income streams by taking out **credit** and borrowing. Debt repayments will, of course, reduce future consumption levels, and will be influenced by interest rates in credit markets.

To quote John Maynard Keynes, *"the importance of money flows from it being a link between the present and the future."*

● Knowledge: **Economic theories of consumption**

The link between income levels and consumption levels is disputed by economists.

● Absolute income hypothesis
John Maynard Keynes argued that national income is the key determinant of consumption. Thus when income levels rise, as in a boom, households will spend more money on goods and services. During a recession, consumption will fall. However, the proportion of income used for consumption may differ. Keynes identified the average propensity to consume (APC) and marginal propensity to consume (MPC) as important features of macroeconomics. The Keynesian model also distinguishes between **autonomous consumption** (spending on necessities) and **induced** or **discretionary consumption** (spending on non-essentials). Only discretionary consumption, in this model, is directly related to income.

● Life cycle hypothesis
Franco Modigliani argued that households smooth out their spending over their lifetimes. At the beginning of people's careers consumption exceeds income as households take out credit to pay for housing and consumer durables. This is known as **dissaving**, or negative saving. In their middle years, workers pay off debt (e.g. mortgages) and begin to save for old age (positive saving). Later in life, these savings can be used to fund consumption in retirement.

● Permanent income hypothesis
Milton Friedman argued that households have a 'permanent income': a rate of return based on ownership of assets (physical assets such as property, and financial assets such as stocks and bonds) and human wealth (skills, education and experience). Short-run shocks, such as redundancy, will not have a major impact on consumption as workers will expect to be re-employed in the future. Only changes to assets and human wealth will affect the permanent income. This is linked to the 'rational expectations' model, where

economic agents take all available information into account and their behaviour is not easily influenced by short-run fluctuations in income or changes in government policy.

● Confidence hypothesis

The role of confidence and expectations are important in economics. Both terms imply an opinion or outlook on the future. In periods when consumer confidence is high, households might choose to consume more and save less as a proportion of their income. When confidence is low, households may increase their saving ratio in preparation for possible falls in income.

● Relative income hypothesis

James Duesenberry argued that consumer spending is determined by cultural as well as economic factors. Households base spending decisions on previous levels (in particular, past 'peak income') and in comparison with other households. Thus low income households consume a higher proportion of their income (and save a lower proportion) to maintain a standard of living similar to that of richer households. This theory helps explain why households may continue to spend even when income has fallen drastically, such as during a period of unemployment in a recession or after retirement.

● Behavioural models

Behavioural economics is a relatively new branch of economics which is concerned with why economic agents might sometimes behave irrationally and make decisions which appear to be less than optimal. Such economists might argue that consumption levels will fluctuate according to the ability of households to defer gratification, which might give important insight into why some people are prone to indebtedness. Other research has suggested that households treat different sources of income in different ways ('mental accounting'). For example, a large 'windfall' income (such as an unexpected bonus or a lottery win) will increase consumption, whereas a small windfall may be saved.

Question

1. What reasons do each of these models suggest for a less than perfect link between consumer spending and income levels?

● ● Application and Analysis: Explaining changes in consumer spending and saving in the UK

Figure 2.1: Growth in UK households' consumer spending

Source: HM Treasury

Figure 2.1 shows the trend in consumer spending growth year on year from 2003 to 2015. Clearly, the impact of recession in 2008 and 2009 can be seen on the chart, as can the drop in confidence when the recovery stalled in 2011. Between 2012 and 2015 growing confidence contributed to economic recovery.

Consumer spending growth has remained strong despite the 'headwinds' of austerity and the uncertainty created by the surprise 'Leave' result in the EU referendum.

The factors which are most likely to explain recent trends in consumer spending are explored below.

1. Rising real disposable incomes

Figure 2.2 shows consumer spending against real GDP since 2007. There is a clear correlation between these two trends, suggesting that national income has a strong influence on household spending.

Figure 2.2: UK real GDP versus household expenditure

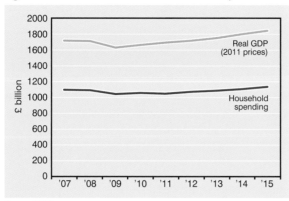

Source: HM Treasury

It should also be noted that consumption growth has played a significant role in fuelling the boom (and bust) in the UK economy in recent years. To suggest that higher consumption led to rising national income, which in turn increased consumption, is a circular argument. It is therefore important to consider other factors which have affected both consumer spending and national income in this period.

2. Interest rates

Interest rates are a cornerstone of monetary policy (see Chapter 9) and they are used by central banks to influence consumption, investment and export performance. Interest rates affect both the incentive to save and the cost of borrowing, and thus should have a strong impact on household's spending decisions.

Put simply, higher interest rates increase the reward to savers and increase the cost of borrowing. This should increase the saving ratio and reduce consumption on goods more likely to be purchased using credit (housing, and consumer durables such as furniture and cars). Falling interest rates should boost consumer spending by reducing the incentive to save and reducing debt repayments.

Figure 2.3: UK base rate and saving ratio

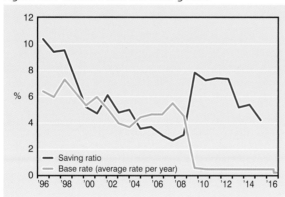

Source: HM Treasury

The link between the base rate and saving ratio is shown in Figure 2.3. In theory, the data should show a positive correlation, but this is not the case. Even with the base rate at a historic low of 0.5% since 2009, the saving ratio has increased considerably from 3% to over 7% during this period. Also, the general upward trend in the base rate between 2003 and 2007 saw the saving ratio almost halve from 5% to less than 3%. It is too early to tell if the further cut in the base rate to 0.25% in August 2016 will reduce saving even further.

One analysis of the period 2003 to 2007 is that interest rates were relatively high but historically low (see Figure 1.19 in Chapter 1). The impact of interest rates on other macroeconomic variables needs to be considered, for example on the exchange rate and the housing market as these will also have influenced household spending.

3. The effect of wealth

Theories such as the Keynesian absolute income hypothesis stress the importance of current income as a determinant of consumption. However, household finances are influenced by wealth as well as income.

● Income is a **flow** concept: it represents earnings over a given period of time, for example an annual salary for a worker or a monthly rent for a landlord.

● Wealth is a **stock** concept: it represents a value of financial worth at a period of time, for example the value of a property or a share in a company.

Wealth can be affected by increases in asset values, most typically resulting from a boom in the housing market or stock market.

2003 saw massive house price inflation as we noted in Chapter 1. Figure 1.15 showed 22.4% on the Halifax index and 19.4% on the Nationwide index. This large increase represented a significant boost to perceived household wealth. The UK housing market was also experiencing a buy-to-let boom, with many people choosing to divert savings from more traditional financial assets (savings accounts and pension funds) and into second homes, which would then provide an income stream (rent) in addition to an increase in value.

2003 saw a more difficult year for the stock market. The FTSE index fell by over 10% as oil prices increased and concerns grew surrounding conflict in the Middle East and tension in North Korea. However, even as the UK housing market cooled, the FTSE bounced back and recorded double-digit gains until the recession of 2008-09.

Figure 2.4: Halifax house price index and FTSE all share index

Source: HM Treasury

The housing market has a particularly powerful effect on the economy in the UK. Unlike other countries in Europe, the UK has a high proportion of owner occupied homes, with at least 50% of homes owner occupied in all regions. This makes consumption more responsive to changes in interest rates (via the impact on mortgage repayments) and to changes in house prices (via wealth effects – positive when house prices rise, but negative when house prices fall).

The debate over the influence of house prices on the wider economy is controversial. If house prices fall, this reduces the wealth of home owners, but it will also reduce the cost of borrowing for first time buyers which in theory leaves more disposable income for other areas of spending. In addition, lower house prices represent a lower cost to landlords in the buy-to-let sector, which according to market theory should reduce the cost of renting and again increase consumption on non-housing goods.

A final consideration is that of mortgage **equity withdrawal**. A homeowner experiencing positive equity (where the market price of their home is greater than the value of mortgage debt outstanding) can, in theory, remortgage their house to free up funds for spending. This can be used for consumption or the purchase of another property for own use or to lease for rental income.

During the NICE decade, the concept of the housing market as a source of extra income and a means of saving for retirement became widespread. This was exacerbated by various factors:

● High house price inflation, outstripping returns from more traditional savings.

● Price inelastic supply of housing in urban areas.

● Demographic changes, increasing the proportion of one-person households.

● A severe decline in confidence in pension schemes after high-profile scandals such as Mirror Group (1991) and Equitable Life (2004).

● A significant increase in global money supply which led to easy credit terms, banks' acceptance of rising loan-to-value ratios, and low interest rates which discouraged saving and reduced borrowing rates.

● Income elastic demand for housing as it is seen as a superior alternative to the 'inferior' good of renting a home.

4. Other factors

The impact of globalisation on the UK economy was an important factor during the NICE decade and beyond. Related issues including migration, greater interconnectedness of international trade and the continued rise of the multinational corporation all played their part in shaping opportunities and threats for UK households, firms and the government.

Key impacts of globalisation have been:

- Cheaper money in world credit markets due to higher saving ratios in emerging economies such as China.

- Falling prices of consumer durables due to lower labour and land costs for growing businesses in Newly Industrialising Countries (NICs), and lower costs for UK-based firms engaging in *off-shoring* (moving business functions to cheaper countries) and *outsourcing* (contracting business functions to be supplied by a cheaper, foreign supplier).

- Greater migration, both into (immigration) and out of (emigration) the UK; this has helped to fill skills gaps in the UK labour market and to offer opportunities for some UK workers to move abroad.

As of late 2016, the future of globalisation itself looks uncertain, as democratic decisions in the UK and USA throw into question the assumption that free trade can, and is accepted to, increase the prosperity of all citizens in developed economies.

Government policy can also influence consumption levels in the economy. Monetary policy clearly influences the key decision whether to spend or save for households and firms, but fiscal policy also affects the incentives to work, earn, save and invest through marginal rates of income tax, tax relief on pension saving, and corporation tax and tax breaks for firms.

Question

2. Using the data given above, which model – or combination of models – provides the most accurate theory of what factors influence consumer spending in the economy?

Analysis: The 'Great Recession': why did consumer spending collapse in 2008-2009?

As noted in Chapter 1 consumer spending is the single largest component of GDP, and it is therefore no surprise that the fall in GDP experienced during the recession of 2008-09 can be largely explained by a drop in consumption. The relationship between consumption, GDP and investment can be analysed by two effects: the multiplier and the accelerator. When economic growth begins to slow, this influences both consumer and business confidence and households and firms change their expectations of future income levels. Investment – capital spending by firms – often responds more quickly and more drastically. Firms do not need to invest; supermarket chains expecting tougher trading conditions can call a halt to expansion, and manufacturers and construction firms will reduce output in anticipation of lower demand. This is called the **accelerator effect**, and is often a key indicator that an economy is heading into recession even before consumers and governments change their behaviour.

Households tend to react more slowly to changes in economic circumstance. The various economic theories of consumption explained in the section at the beginning of this chapter show that the correlation between income, and income expectations, and consumer spending is not perfect. However, a drop in investment (or a fall in other injections into the circular flow, such as government spending or net exports) reduces GDP, in turn affecting household's abilities to afford to maintain existing standards of living. The recession of 2008-09 was in many ways a casebook in how recession leads to falling consumer spending, with the addition of some other factors which compounded the problems already facing households.

● Falling disposable incomes

However imperfect, the link between spending and earnings is nonetheless important. Recession led to rising unemployment, directly reducing average earnings, and even workers who remained in employment often faced wage freezes and lower bonuses and commission than had been available during the previous boom. In addition, CPI inflation remained stubbornly high despite negative growth, eroding the real value of incomes as prices increased faster than average earnings.

● Negative wealth effects

The housing market experienced dramatic 'corrections' as the bubble burst. Despite unprecedented reductions in the base rate of interest, which reduced the burden of debt on owner-occupiers with variable mortgage repayments, households experienced a reduction in wealth as the market value of their homes fell. This was exacerbated by the inflow of funds into the buy-to-let market during 'the NICE decade', and was matched by losses in stock market values which further reduced the wealth and confidence of households.

● Tougher credit conditions

Despite reductions in the base rate of interest by the Bank of England, the actual costs of financing credit cards and mortgages rose. Banks became less willing to lend as they attempted to address the bad debts on their books, and when lending was available the risk premium was often increased to reflect the difficult trading conditions in the financial sector. This disconnection between the base rate and market rates of interest was known as '**decoupling**', and raises serious questions about the effectiveness of monetary policy in managing demand during a credit crisis.

● Higher saving ratio

Figure 2.5: UK saving ratio

Source: HM Treasury

Despite falling incomes, downturn and recession is often accompanied by an increase in the saving ratio as households increase precautionary balances in case of job losses, and also to try to bring down debt levels if they predict negative equity on their home. Figure 2.5 shows this effect clearly. The problem is further compounded as consumers reduce their discretionary spending (purchasing of non-essential goods and services), leading to lower demand and job losses for suppliers of these 'luxury' goods.

● Commodity price rises

Prices of oil and food products increased in 2008, reducing the ability of households to buy other goods and services. Low income households in particular are affected significantly by higher food and energy prices. More recently, the price of foods and energy had fallen globally, but the drastic depreciation in sterling since June 2016 is likely to put upward pressure on prices of imported goods in the UK.

Question

3. What is meant by the terms 'food poverty' and 'fuel poverty' in an economy such as the UK? Why are these problems of greater significance during recession?

● ● Application and Analysis: Explaining changes in the pattern of saving in the UK

Perhaps counter-intuitively, between 1995 and 2008 (except for a few minor increases) UK households saved a falling proportion of incomes. However, once the economy entered recession, the ratio increased by 250%, from 2% to 7% by 2010. Clearly, the concept of a stable **average propensity** or **marginal propensity to save** is highly dubious.

The different reasons for saving are important to explore at this stage.

Households save to defer present consumption and fund future consumption (e.g. saving for a future holiday or to buy high-price consumer durables, or when waiting for prices to fall), to prepare for retirement (e.g. saving in a pension fund), and as a means of avoiding future drops in consumption if income expectations are uncertain (precautionary saving). It is this latter factor which best explains the UK saving ratio over the last 15 years.

In times of strong economic growth, and when households expect such growth to continue, households may save a lower proportion of income as the need to build up precautionary balances declines. In essence, households believe they are less likely to be jobless, and thus feel free to spend a higher proportion of what they earn.

Other factors also reduced the saving ratio up to 2007:

- Historically low interest rates encouraged borrowing and discouraged saving in the UK.

- Relatively high interest rates pushed up the value of sterling and pushed down the prices of imported goods, helping to fuel a consumer boom.

- Rising house prices increased positive equity in property, reducing the need for households to save income to build up wealth levels.

During the 'Great Recession' of 2008-09 the rise in the saving ratio can perhaps be best explained by the precautionary saving model.

- Low consumer and business confidence and a weak labour market made households wary of spending and more inclined to save due to the threat of unemployment. Despite very low rates of return, saving has increased as a proportion of income.

- Households with high levels of indebtedness (most significantly where large loans were taken out to buy housing at peak prices in 2007) may seek to pay down debt levels to reduce their exposure to negative equity. This is known as a '**balance sheet recession**', or '**debt hangover**': even where positive income growth has resumed, economic agents feel a negative wealth effect through property and other asset prices remaining below their previous peak.

● Knowledge: **The paradox of thrift – should more saving be encouraged?**

John Maynard Keynes popularised the concept of the **paradox of thrift**; that every decision to save, rather than spend, reduces demand in the economy and therefore causes demand-deficient unemployment. This is encapsulated by the quote, 'Whenever you save five shillings, you put a man out of work for a day.'

However, the then Governor of the Bank of England, Mervyn King, said in 2009 that, 'the United Kingdom faces… fundamental long-run challenge(s)… to rebalance the economy, with more resources allocated to business investment and net exports and fewer to consumption. That is consistent with the need – now widely accepted – to eliminate the large structural fiscal deficit and to raise the national saving rate.'[1]

The paradox of thrift appears to suggest that higher saving will reduce demand and reduce economic growth further. However, this assumes that higher savings create only lower demand, and are not used to create extra borrowing, which in turn stimulates purchases of consumer durables and business investment. The efficiency of the financial industry in creating credit is therefore an important factor in determining whether the higher saving ratio in recent years has been harmful or not. In the same speech quoted above, Mervyn King proposed the second challenge facing the UK was to reform the structure and regulation of the banking sector. He later made calls for banks to lend more money to smaller businesses, providing essential credit for firms to expand and create jobs and profit.

---

1. http://www.bankofengland.co.uk/publications/Documents/speeches/2009/speech406.pdf

Question

4. Does it matter if the savings ratio of UK households continues to fall?

● Analysis: **The Pensions Crisis: an even bigger problem?**

As important a role as savings play in the success of the macroeconomy, one area of concern in many highly developed economies is that of pension provision. A pension is a saving device to allow households to put money aside during their working years to fund retirement. Traditionally, workers would be employed by only a small number of firms (and often only one) over their working life, and powerful trade unions negotiated generous pensions based on final salary. The state pension – payments to old age pensioners, regardless of household income and wealth – was also an important element of the welfare state since 1945.

Various factors have created a potential pension crisis for the UK:

● Increased life expectancy (Figure 2.6).

● For some years, the UK experienced a falling birth rate (Figure 2.7).

● Increased numbers of people extending their education past the compulsory school-leaving age, meaning later entry into the labour market.

● These two factors have also contributed to a shift towards families having children at a later age, leading to 'generational stretch' (Figure 2.8 shows the proportion of births to mothers over the age of 40 has risen four-fold since 1980).

● Greater labour market mobility and a breakdown of the 'job for life' culture has increased the likely number of employers in a worker's lifetime – reducing the ability of workers to build up a substantial pension saving.

● Loss of confidence in traditional pension schemes.

● Higher yields from other forms of 'saving', such as the buy-to-let market during the housing boom in the second half of the NICE decade.

● Lower interest rates for savers, especially since the drastic cuts in the base rate in 2009.

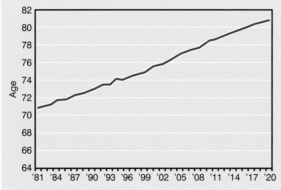

Figure 2.6: UK life expectancy at birth (2012-20 projections)

Source: ONS

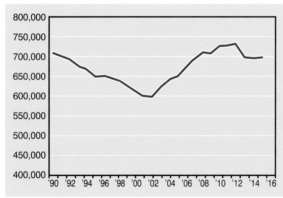

Figure 2.7: UK births (p.a.)

Source: ONS

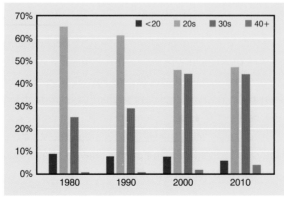

Figure 2.8: Births by age of mother (as % of births p.a.)

Source: ONS

European countries where a 'pensions timebomb' is predicted to take place during the 21st century include the UK, Italy and Spain. A combination of high youth unemployment, high housing costs and a shift in culture away from 'traditional' family values may leave the economy short of workers (and therefore tax-payers) at a time when the cost of supporting an ageing population rises dramatically, given improvements in healthcare and rising life expectancies.

Figure 2.7 shows that, for the UK, the number of births has actually been rising since 2001. Some of this is due to greater immigration and higher birth rates in migrant families.

Policies which could be used to tackle the pensions timebomb problem include:

● Higher state pension retirement age (the age at which a state pension can be collected).

● Means-tested state pension (higher income households – typically those with significant private pensions – will no longer receive state pensions).

● Less generous state pension payments in real terms.

● Greater incentives to save for a pension, e.g. higher tax relief on employee and employer contributions.

● Extensive public information campaigns to alert young workers to the importance of preparing for retirement.

● Greater labour market flexibility to allow older workers to remain working, perhaps in part-time or flexible capacities.

● Compulsory employer pension contributions. In fact, by 2018 it will be compulsory for all employers to offer most workers a pension scheme.

● A minimum retirement age for private as well as state pension funds.

● A 'laissez-faire' approach, where older workers who have not saved sufficiently will have no choice but to continue working or depend on other benefits, e.g. disability or sickness payments.

● Compulsory individual pension tax (this has been introduced in Australia).

The pension issue is a very good example of how long-term problems which require long-term solutions are often ignored by governments of the day. **Public choice theory** suggests that governments do not, in reality, aim to maximise social welfare, but rather seek re-election by 'buying' votes with policies which appeal to their core electorate. The likely popularity of the policies listed above offers an insight into the likelihood of core reforms taking place before more drastic decisions have to be made.

One important point to consider is whether these projected increases in life expectancy will actually occur. Highly developed societies may actually see health outcomes worsen due to factors such as stress, sedentary lifestyles, and high-fat diets. However, the worse case scenario for the public finances would be an increase in healthcare costs for the obese and unhealthy, but a continued rise in life expectancy: people could stay sicker for longer while unable to work, with drastic negative impacts on NHS and care costs.

Extension Question

5. The Australian government introduced a compulsory 'pension tax' in the 1990s.

   Evaluate the case for and against such a policy in the UK.

Chapter 3

Business and Industry

● ● **Knowledge and Application: The structure of the UK economy**

The term **economic growth** refers to increases in the productive capacity of an economy: how increases in the quantity and quality of factors of production can lead to higher output levels and a rising standard of living.

Over the past 300 years, the structure of the UK economy has undergone radical change. Modern economies such as the UK have typically experienced a series of 'revolutions' during which the dominant industries for employment and output have changed dramatically.

1. Industrial revolution

As new technologies in the *primary sector* (agricultural and energy extraction industries) developed, this liberated some land, labour and capital for use in the emerging *secondary sector* (manufacturing). Large numbers of households moved from the countryside to towns and cities to work in factories and mills. Thus **industrialisation** occurred alongside **urbanisation** and the manufacturing sector grew in importance throughout the 19th and 20th centuries. In terms of the agricultural sector, by 2012 60% of the UK's food needs were produced domestically by less than 2% of the workforce.

2. Post-industrial revolution

By the 1970s and 1980s, it was clear that the UK manufacturing sector was facing increasing competition from the resurgent economies of Germany and Japan, other trading partners within the expanding European Economic Community (the precursor to today's European Union) and from newly-industrialising countries such as Taiwan. The process of **deindustrialisation** saw British manufacturing face serious decline, as either UK-based firms moved production overseas, were driven out of business, or were absorbed into multinational conglomerates through merger or takeover.

Between 1997 and 2007, manufacturing output in the UK fell from 28% to 12% of GDP and manufacturing employment fell from one in four workers to one in ten. These changes were almost perfectly matched by an equivalent growth in service sector output and employment. However, as of 2009 the manufacturing sector employed 2.6 million British workers and the UK remained the world's sixth largest exporter by value of output, and a major exporter of technology-intensive manufactures. By 2000 the main threat to the UK's competitiveness in global manufacturing markets was the rapidly developing economies of China and India.

Figure 3.1: Growth in industrial production, selected economies

Source: HM Treasury

Figure 3.1 shows how UK industrial production growth compares with other regions and countries in recent years.

Clearly, all four of the economies shown in Figure 3.1 saw manufacturing output fall during the recession of 2008-09. The UK saw the lowest fall in output of those economies shown, but throughout the pre-recession period of 2001-07 the UK had the lowest average rate of growth (a contraction of 0.4%, compared with growth in the USA of 1.2%, 1.3% in Japan and 2.8% in Germany).

Figure 3.2: Growth in industrial production, UK, compared with the G7 average

Source: HM Treasury

Figure 3.2 compares UK industrial growth with the G7 average. (The G7 group of countries comprises Canada, France, Germany, Italy, Japan, the USA and the UK.) Figure 3.2 shows that except for 2009, the G7 average growth rate outstripped growth in the UK economy.

Data for G7 industrial output growth in 2014 and 2015 was unavailable at the time of publication.

● Analysis: Why has the UK experienced deindustrialisation?

Reasons for the decline in the importance of UK manufacturing within the UK and in global markets include:

● Loss of competitive advantage against lower-cost producers, including **newly-industrialising countries** (**NIC**s) such as China, Taiwan, South Korea and Singapore.

● Loss of competitive advantage against other advanced economies. As Figure 3.3 shows, the UK's productivity performance compares unfavourably with the EU since 2010.

● Increasingly globalised markets for traded goods which reduced transport costs to facilitate greater world trade.

● Relatively high land costs in the UK (linked to higher population density in urban areas).

Figure 3.3: The UK productivity gap – EU minus UK annual productivity growth.

Source: OECD

● Relatively high labour costs in the UK (strong trade union power until the 1980s, and a higher standard of living and therefore higher cost of living).

● Weak investment in infrastructure, reducing the efficiency of national and international trading links.

● The economist Jim O'Neill, of Goldman Sachs, has identified the new wave of NICs known as the MINT economies: Mexico, Indonesia, Nigeria and Turkey

● Evaluation: Is manufacturing still important in the UK?

The period of strong growth in the UK between the mid-1990s and 2007 was characterised by high levels of consumer demand, increased government expenditure, a falling saving ratio and a widening trade imbalance, as imports into the UK outstripped exports from the UK at a growing rate.

In May 2011, the Governor of the Bank of England, Mervyn King, was quoted as saying, *"The rebalancing of the UK economy which implies slow growth in consumer spending and in public spending will take not just one year but several years, and the switch to business investment and net exports will also take several years."*[1]

---

1. http://www.bbc.co.uk/blogs/thereporters/stephanieflanders/2011/05/inflation_up_growth_down_uncer.html

In common with many mature economies, the UK has experienced an expanding tertiary (service) sector as the secondary (manufacturing) sector has shrunk. This section will explore the key question: is the decline of manufacturing important?

The relevant factors to consider in answering this question include the following:

- Manufactured goods are easier to export than (most) services. The UK enjoys a strong position as a major provider of financial services such as banking and insurance and is also a major tourism destination (ranked sixth in the world) but other services are produced for predominantly domestic consumption, such as transport, healthcare and retail.

- Chapter 5, which examines the current account of the balance of payments, offers more detail regarding the balance of internationally traded goods and services. Trade in services has been in surplus (exports from the UK have exceeded imports into the UK) over every one of the past 20 years, whereas the trade in goods has been in deficit. It is important to note that the services surplus has been smaller than the goods deficit – a major contributor to the current account deficit in recent years.

- A shrinking manufacturing sector can also explain a relative decline in UK productivity. Technological innovation can increase productivity, usually by allowing labour (which can be expensive in a country such as the UK, where the cost of living is high) for cheaper capital (which, in the present century, can increasingly be produced in low-wage, low-rent NICs). Such substitution, however, is more difficult in the service sector industries where the UK enjoys a competitive advantage, such as tourism or financial services. Figure 3.4 shows productivity growth in manufacturing compared with services.

Figure 3.4: Productivity in UK manufacturing and service sectors (index, 2006 = 100)

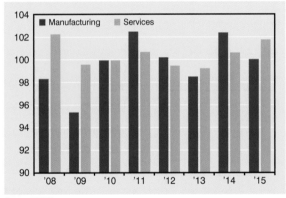

Source: HM Treasury

- A strong manufacturing sector can also stimulate a culture of innovation and investment. This is linked to the point above: the possibility of high returns from capital spending acts as an incentive for firms to spend on research and development (R&D) which can be a key driver of long-run, supply-side growth for the macroeconomy.

- Finally, manufacturing still accounts for 60% of the value of UK exports. The pattern of exports of goods from the UK (see Figure 3.5) gives a clear indication of the competitiveness and value of the manufacturing sectors of the UK economy.

- The UK clearly still enjoys a strong position as an exporter of manufactured goods such as cars. In addition, manufacturing activity creates jobs in related service sector industries such as transport, distribution and finance.

Figure 3.5: UK exports by industry (goods) £bn, 2014

Cars	$46.0 bn	(9.7% of value of UK exports)
Gold	$37.4 bn	(7.9%)
Crude petroleum	$23.1 bn	(4.9%)
Refined petroleum	$22.1 bn	(4.7%)
Gas turbines	$15.3 bn	(3.2%)

There are wider arguments regarding the importance, and even desirability, of sustaining UK manufacturing to consider.

● Export-led growth may not improve the current account position significantly if UK production depends on imported raw materials or even, in some cases, off-shored and outsourced production and services.

● Policies to boost UK production of manufactures may distort the market and lead to resources being wasted on relatively expensive and relatively low quality goods.

● A trade deficit in goods need not be a problem providing earnings from services, investment income and transfers are sufficient to create an overall balance on the current account. Thus support which might be given to the manufacturing sector might be more efficiently utilised in bolstering already strong competitive advantages in service sector industries.

● Arguably, structural shifts in the UK economy moving production away from manufacturing and towards services represent strong market forces which the UK and its policy-makers are powerless to totally resist. It is likely that even if a resurgence in large scale manufacturing were to take place in the UK (however unlikely) this would create more jobs for robots than for humans.

Question

1. What factors could explain why service sector productivity growth may differ from that in manufacturing?

●● Knowledge and Application: Investment in the UK

Figure 3.6: UK investment (% of GDP)

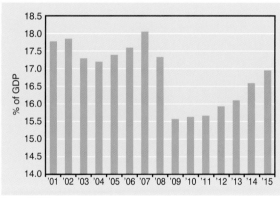

Source: HM Treasury

Investment plays a crucial role in any economy. As a significant component of aggregate demand, investment spending contributes to GDP and therefore the overall health of the macroeconomy through creating output and jobs. Investment is also a key driver of long-run trend growth, increasing productivity and productive potential.

Investment has formed an increasing share of GDP in recent years, but is still below the levels experienced before the Great Recession.

● Analysis: Why is investment volatile?

Investment levels in the economy are seen by economists as an important indicator of the future expectations of firms. If business confidence is strong, firms are prepared to commit spending to increasing their production and supply potential. But when confidence is weak they will stop new investment projects (and even in extreme cases, mothball current projects) as they anticipate flat or falling demand in the future. Figure 3.7 shows the annual percentage change in investment levels in the UK. Investment spending tends to be more volatile than other components of GDP, such as consumption and government spending, for various reasons:

● The accelerator effect

Investment spending often reacts more quickly and more dramatically than spending by households and the public sector. This was discussed in more detail in Chapter 2, where causes of the fall in consumer

Figure 3.7: UK investment

Source: HM Treasury

spending in 2008-09 are discussed. In brief, firms can reduce investment more easily than households can do with consumer spending. A high proportion of household consumption, particularly for those on lower incomes, is called **autonomous consumption**. Mortgage payments or rent, and spending on food and energy are difficult to change in the short-run without significant adjustments to lifestyles, and therefore even when average incomes fall in the economy there may be a period where household spending does not keep up with this change.

Similarly, governments are committed to both **current spending** (public sector wages and other running costs) and **capital spending** (public sector investment in infrastructure and nationalised sectors). Capital projects can, of course, be mothballed, but for reasons of demand-management this may be a difficult policy to implement particularly when economic growth is falling or even negative.

● Rates of return

Investment has to be paid for, and firms will generally do this by either borrowing money from a bank, issuing corporate bonds or using previous profits (retained profit).

The rate of interest charged by banks can vary according to changes in monetary policy and the competitiveness and health of the financial sector. Since the credit crisis of 2007, many small and medium sized firms in the UK have complained that credit is difficult to find, and interest rates are too high. Similarly, the rate of return offered on corporate bonds will be determined by both prevailing returns, or rates of interest in the credit markets, as well as the appetite bond purchasers have for risk.

● Retained profits

An alternative to borrowing is to fund business expansion from the profits accrued in previous years. Retained profit is likely to be higher during the boom stage of the economic cycle, which explains why investment can rise so dramatically during a period of rapid economic expansion.

● Technology

It is important to distinguish between **gross profit** and **net profit**. Gross profit is simply total spending on capital goods by firms over a given period of time. However, this will include some of what economists call **depreciation**: the replacement of worn-out or obsolete equipment. If a high proportion of gross investment goes to replace rather than expand production facilities, this will not increase the productive capacity of the firm (and, indeed, the economy) as much as the data might suggest. Net investment is the term used for the overall change in productive capacity, and is calculated as gross investment minus depreciation.

Question

2. In periods of rapid technological change, such as the industrial revolution, explain why investment might be high. Also, why might net investment be considerably lower?

●● Knowledge and Application: Foreign Direct Investment

Foreign Direct Investment (FDI) refers to cross-border investment activities by **multinational companies** (**MNC**s). FDI can be outward (where UK firms invest in plant overseas) or inward (where foreign firms invest in the UK). Global FDI levels shrank from $1.9 trillion in 2007 to $1.35 in 2012. FDI varies according to activity and confidence levels in the national and international economy. The impact of the credit crisis and Great Recession can be seen in Figures 3.6 and 3.7. A pressing question for the UK is to what extent the Brexit decision will affect FDI inflows in the years ahead; this is explored in greater detail below and in Chapter 11.

Figure 3.8: Inward FDI to the UK

Source: ONS

The factors attracting FDI into the UK are explored further below.

● Analysis: Why is FDI important?

The advantages of FDI for the UK are:

- Inwards FDI is an injection into the circular flow of income and thus creates output and jobs, both directly and indirectly through the supply chain.
- This economic activity will create tax revenues for the UK government from VAT and income taxes.
- The inflow of funds contributes to the UK's surplus on the financial account of the balance of payments.
- Multinationals bring new knowledge and technology to the UK, creating higher productivity gains which can spill over into domestic firms.

The disadvantages of FDI for the UK are:

- Profits made in the UK by a foreign firm may be repatriated to the head office, which is likely to be overseas. MNCs with interests in the UK may therefore pay no or very little corporation tax to the Treasury. Repatriated profits, and earnings by foreign executives living in the UK, will be a debit on the financial account of the balance of payments.
- Foreign firms compete with domestic firms, which may lead to job losses (particularly if the MNC enjoys higher productivity and the economies of scale associated with large organisations).
- MNCs aim to maximise profits, and therefore will choose to operate in economies where the tax regime is favourable to the firm and its employees. It can be argued, therefore, that attempts to maintain FDI can constrain domestic fiscal policy, such as a specific levy on banking.
- MNCs are mobile, or 'footloose', and may therefore leave whenever trading conditions determine they might be more profitably located elsewhere. This can cause structural unemployment, which is usually geographically concentrated.

● Analysis: Will the UK remain an attractive destination for FDI?

The non-inflationary growth of the NICE decade and the acceptance of the importance of globalisation by the New Labour government made the UK one of the main recipients of FDI in recent years (25% of inward FDI in the EU; the UK was second to only the USA as the largest recipient of global FDI in 1998).

Other factors making the UK attractive are:

- High lender of consumer spending (a large 'host market').
- A highly-skilled labour force, particularly in financial services and some high technology manufacturing sectors.

- Membership of the European Union, meaning any output exported from the UK to other EU countries is classed as a British export and therefore is not subject to the Common External Tariff (import tax).
- The UK labour market is more flexible and lightly regulated than in many other European economies, making it easier and cheaper for MNCs to recruit workers here.

Other factors which can increase inward FDI are agglomeration effects ('clusters' of economic activity which attract related and complementary firms, such as hi-tech industries and tourism) and imperfect competition (the potential for monopoly power implies higher future profits, provided barriers to entry to the sector can be maintained).

The recession in 2008 then led to considerably reduced inward FDI in 2009 before recovering later, possibly because these challenging macroeconomic conditions were experienced throughout the EU and the UK remained an attractive place to invest. Relative to the performance of 'the PIIGS' (Portugal, Ireland, Italy, Greece and Spain), the UK has arguably gained a competitive advantage. By 2015, the UK had become the third most attractive target country for FDI (behind USA and China).

Economists have assumed that an economy's position inside the single market and customs union has made it an attractive destination for FDI, and the impact of the UK's decision to leave is both uncertain, and highly significant for future patterns of cross-border investment. Tariff-free access to the EU's single market is one of the factors behind, for example, Japanese car manufacturers locating in the UK.

The UK attracts FDI from over 70 countries and territories, as shown in Table 3.1. Until the Brexit negotiations are complete and the UK has left the EU, the future pattern of UK FDI will be difficult to predict.

However, it is possible that the UK will remain attractive to overseas firms:

- The UK has relatively low levels of corporation tax which are being lowered from 20% to 19% in 2017 and to 17% from 2020.
- The UK has a 'central' time zone which allows same-day trading with North American and Asian markets; however, other European regions also enjoy this advantage.
- The international business language is English; this, alongside the relatively stable business environment and political system make areas of the UK highly attractive to expat workers and their families.
- The UK will be more open to global trade and may be able to negotiate favourable trading deals with any number of other economies and trading blocs.

Table 3.1: Top source markets for FDI projects in the UK, and impact on jobs (2014-15)

Source market	Number of projects	New jobs	Safeguarded jobs
USA	564	26,505	10,273
France	124	5,584	2,614
India	122	7,730	1,620
China (inc. Hong Kong)	112	4,728	1,199
Japan	107	3,256	617
Germany	97	8,950	777
Italy	91	1,251	942
Australia	81	3,998	14
Canada	72	3,557	205
Rest of world	631	21,828	4,942

Source: gov.uk

Questions
3. Using Table 3.1, what do you think is the difference between a 'new job' and 'safeguarded job' resulting from FDI into the UK?

4. What does the data in Table 3.1 suggest about the pattern of FDI coming into the UK in 2014-15?

● ● Knowledge **and** Application: **The UK stock market**

The performance of the UK stock market in recent years was shown in Figure 1.11 in Chapter 1. The stock market offers an insight into the performance of the largest firms in the economy, most of which have publicly-owned shares. These shares (which are a *share* of ownership, and entitle holders to a *share* of the profits made) are traded on the stock market. Aggregate measures such as the FTSE indices show how the values of those firms are changing, based mainly on their fundamental ability to generate future profits. Therefore we might expect stock market performance to correlate closely with overall macroeconomic performance, measured best as real GDP growth. Figure 3.8 shows the movement in real GDP growth in the UK with the annual change in stock market prices.

Figure 3.8: Real GDP growth and stock market performance for the UK

Source: HM Treasury

Stock market volatility tends to be far greater than growth volatility. This trend has persisted throughout history, and was named 'animal spirits' by John Maynard Keynes: a form of herd behaviour where speculators over-react to the potential gains, and losses, in rapidly changing asset markets. This can be contrasted with the 'wisdom of crowds' theory, where aggregate opinions and behaviours are seen as more perceptive and rational than individual decisions.

The '**bull markets**' of 1996-2000 and 2004-07 can be viewed with hindsight as examples of stock market bubbles, and fit into the wider picture presented in Chapter 1 of a period of very high consumption growth in the UK, fuelled by wealth effects from the housing market and stock markets. When UK (and global) growth appeared to falter after the 2000 dot-com crash, the UK stock market fell dramatically (this is known as a '**bear market**'), before recovering strongly in the years before the credit crisis and recession at the end of the 2000s.

Interestingly, the percentage loss experienced on the FTSE index in 2002 was just as severe as that seen in 2008, when the UK economy was in recession. At the end of 2003 the FTSE All Share Index stood at less than 2000, compared with 2329 in December 2009 and 3427 in December 2013.

Stock markets had increased steadily through 2013 and 2014 in both the UK and USA but the markets saw significant drops in October 2014 against increasing threats of a Eurozone recession and slowing growth in emerging economies. The Brexit decision in June 2016 sent shockwaves through the global financial system, but stock markets recovered quickly and by November 2016 the FTSE 100 and FTSE 250 indices were higher than 12 months before. The uncertainty in the market for UK stocks has been offset by a significant weakening in the pound, which both improves export prospects for UK firms, and increases the sterling value of revenues generated overseas.

Question
5. Figure 3.8 shows the volatile character of stock market prices compared with growth in the real economy. To explain this greater volatility the stockmarket has been described as "a market not in the present but in the future". How does that description help to account for the contrasting data in Figure 3.8?

Chapter 4
Living Standards, Poverty and Inequality

This chapter examines the changes in living standards over the past decade, looking at various measures of living standards. Measures of inequality and poverty are then examined, along with trends in inequality and poverty over the past decade. Following this there is a discussion on recent government policy to tackle poverty and inequality, concluding with a look at regional differences within the UK.

● Knowledge: **Standard of living**

There is considerable debate amongst economists about how best to measure standard of living. Many factors influence people's living standards. These include social, environmental, and political factors as well as economic ones. However, the vast majority of economists agree that a person or household's income is a very important determinant of living standards. National **income** is the sum of all the earnings received through employing factors of production in a given period of time. Crucially, income is a **flow** of payments. Income to a household could be in the form of wages, salaries, profits, interest payments, rents or other forms of payments received such as state benefits and pensions.

● Application: **The rise and then 'squeeze' on living standards in the last decade**

Figure 4.1: Growth in UK real household disposable income

Source ONS

'Real' household income growth is the growth in household income received accounting for the effects of inflation. Figure 4.1 shows the rate at which the average household's purchasing power has changed over the last 18 years. During the late 1990s in the Labour government's first term in office, real household incomes grew rapidly, but there was a marked slowdown in real income growth from 2002 onwards. Perhaps the most surprising part of Figure 4.1 is that average real household incomes continued to grow during the 'Great Recession' of 2008-09, when GDP and employment fell considerably. During these two years, household incomes were supported by a combination of growth in income from tax credits and state benefits, along with stable employment income and low inflation (according to the RPI index inflation was actually negative in 2009). However, the effects of the recession were delayed, not evaded. As the recovery faltered in 2010 and unemployment rose above 8%, workers had little bargaining power and average wage growth has remained anaemic ever since. Many workers accepted pay cuts or pay freezes. In addition, high cost-push inflationary pressures from rising petrol, food, clothing and energy prices eroded real household incomes. In September 2011 CPI inflation reached 5.2%, but then it fell sharply towards the 2.0% target by mid 2012. From early 2013 the recovery finally took hold and from mid 2014 inflation plummeted, which finally brought some significant growth in real household income.

However, the vote to leave the EU on 23rd June 2016 caused a significant cut in growth forecasts, putting downward pressure on wage growth, and a sharp upturn for inflation is forecast for 2017-18. As a result, real income growth is set to be 'squeezed' once again. Following the Autumn Statement in November 2016, the respected Institute for Fiscal Studies (IFS) said workers would earn less in real wages in 2021 than they did in 2008, representing the biggest 'squeeze' on living standards since the 1920s. Figure 4.2 shows that

Figure 4.2: Real total pay growth, 3 month average, % year on year growth

Source ONS

the Office for Budget Responsibility predicts meagre but positive real total pay growth from 2016 to 2021, but this is one of the more optimistic forecasts.

Explanations of the squeeze on real incomes phenomenon include low productivity growth in the UK, and firms and workers preferring to keep employment levels high instead of raising pay, as they are unwilling to shed talent and lose their investment in training, though there is no consensus. Some also point to the fact that many of the new jobs created in the last 10 years have been low paid, relatively unskilled and often temporary service sector jobs, whereas more productive, better paid manufacturing jobs have been lost due to a comparative disadvantage in trade in manufactures (see Chapter 5), but more importantly the automation of the production process.

Although there are various ways in which living standards can be measured, **real GDP per capita** is the measure most commonly used by economists. There are however, limitations to the use of this measure. These include:

● No account taken for the distribution of income and wealth – GDP per capita is a crude 'mean' measure, and so it might not give an accurate reflection of the income of an 'average' person in a country, especially if income is distributed unevenly. If a large share of national income is concentrated at the top end of the income distribution, then the mean GDP per capita figure will be higher than the true income of the 'average' person. Therefore, a measure of median income might be a better reflection of the income of an 'average' person.

● No account taken for externalities – growth often occurs with resulting negative externalities (e.g. pollution) but these are not accounted for in GDP figures. In fact, the expense of cleaning up pollution may even add *positively* to GDP figures. Thus, growth in GDP may overstate the resultant rise in living standards.

● Quality changes ignored – over time the quality of goods and services tend to increase but these are not accounted for in GDP figures. Therefore, rises in the quality of goods and services (e.g. safer cars, better quality TVs etc.) means that increases in living standards may be greater than a crude GDP per capita measure suggests.

● No account taken for the 'balance' of growth – growth based on consumption today may take available resources away from investment, which would bring faster growth tomorrow. The UK economy has become very dependent on consumption, as mentioned in Chapter 1. Since the financial crisis policy makers have emphasised the importance of a 'rebalancing' of the economy away from consumption and importing, towards investment and exports.

● Exports are valued more highly than imports – In GDP statistics the value of exports is added to GDP while the value of imports is subtracted from GDP, as shown in the formula C + I + G + (X-M). So, according to GDP data imports subtract from living standards, which plainly isn't true in many cases. If UK citizens enjoy a foreign made car, or some fine French wine, in reality this will add to, rather than detract from, living standards.

● No account taken for non-marketed items – if you carry out some DIY work on your home, or someone babysits for you free of charge, these services will not be counted in GDP statistics, but if you pay for these (or similar services), they will be counted.

- No account taken for the opportunity cost of growth – in order to create growth leisure time may be foregone. By working longer hours GDP may increase, but living standards might not.

- Admin errors are likely – GDP data is calculated using tax returns from millions of sources. There are bound to be errors and inaccuracies in the data.

Exam Hint

When answering an exam question it may be relevant to explain some of the limitations of using GDP data to estimate living standards. It is better to go for **depth** over **breadth**. Pick two or three limitations and explain them in detail, rather than explaining five limitations superficially.

Alternative measures to income

The material 'standard of living' can be contrasted with '**quality of life**' which accounts for other, more intangible factors that affect human life, such as health, environmental quality, safety, social life, culture etc. Attempts to measure quality of life intend to give a better indicator of people's overall '**well-being**'.

The **Genuine Progress indicator** (**GPI**) is an extension of the **Index of Sustainable Economic Welfare** (**ISEW**). The GPI aims to account for the costs of the negative consequences of economic growth, as well as the positive impacts, and hence give a more balanced account of how the overall well being of a country's citizens have changed over time. The measure accounts for factors that the GDP measure ignores, such as:

- Cost of resource depletion
- Cost of crime
- Cost of ozone depletion
- Cost of family breakdown
- Cost of air, water, and noise pollution
- Loss of farmland
- Loss of wetlands

With such emphasis placed on environmental as well as social factors, it is unsurprising that the GPI is a popular measure amongst 'green' economists. The ISEW and GPI indicators show a diverging trend from the GDP measure since the 1970s for most rich economies, including the UK. The GPI failed to increase significantly since the 1970s, suggesting that rising incomes since the 1970s has come at the expense of high and unsustainable environmental and social costs, meaning that growth is now failing to add to the well-being of citizens in advanced economies. Of course, accurately measuring the cost of family breakdown and global warming is extremely difficult, and this is something that neo-classical economists point to when defending the GDP measure.

The United Nations first published the **Human Development Index** (**HDI**) in 1990. The HDI is composed of three indicators, and countries are given a score between 0 and 1. The indicators include:

- Real GDP per capita (using Purchasing Power Parity)
- Life expectancy at birth (to indicate the population's level of health and longevity)
- Educational attainment (measured using a weighted average of adult literacy rates and the gross enrolment ratio at primary, secondary and tertiary education level).

In Table 4.1 the final column showing the GDP per capita rank minus the HDI ranking for different countries is one way of examining whether higher incomes result in a higher quality of life for the citizens of that country. So a country with a positive value in the final column has a higher quality of life than its GDP per capita suggests.It is clearly not always the case that this occurs. South Africa has a GDP per capita ranking

39 places higher than its HDI ranking. This is due to the high rates of HIV/AIDS coupled with very high unemployment and poverty rates which reduce life expectancy considerably. Cuba has a low ranking for GDP per capita owing to an inefficient command economy. However, Cuba's HDI ranking is 11 places higher due to an extensive literacy campaign and substantial public investment in healthcare. The UK's performance in the HDI rankings is hindered by a lower average number of years of schooling than other advanced economies.

Table 4.1: Selected HDI and GDP per capita data

Country	HDI value (2013)	HDI ranking	GDP per capita (PPP$) 2012	GDP per capita ranking	GDP per capita – HDI ranking
Norway	0.944	1	62,858	6	5
Australia	0.933	2	42,278	15	13
United States	0.914	5	50,859	9	4
UK	0.892	14	34,694	27	13
South Africa	0.658	118	11,989	79	-39
Cuba	0.815	44	*18,796	55	11
China	0.719	91	10,771	88	-3

Source: UN Human Development Report 2014   *2011

Evaluation of HDI as an indicator of living standards

Advantages	Disadvantages
The HDI goes beyond crude GDP measurements with all the associated limitations to incorporate statistics on education and healthcare, two key development goals.	The HDI is an aggregate measure which hides distribution.
The publishing of this indicator encourages countries to invest in education and healthcare.	Aggregate measures do little to tell us why HDI may have changed over time.
Unlike GDP an element of 'well being' is reflected in the statistics.	Wouldn't quality-adjusted life years (QALYs) be a better measure than simply the average number of years lived?
The HDI does not include too many indices and thus the problem of overlap is avoided e.g. infant mortality is not included but its importance is reflected in the life expectancy indicator.	Shouldn't the quality of education be included, rather than just years in schooling? The UK has some of the best universities in the world, but this is not accounted for in the HDI measure.
The indices used are relatively easy to measure e.g. no value has to be placed on the cost of global warming.	Weightings given (equal for all 3 indicators) are fairly arbitrary. Some argue that income should be given more importance.
The UN now calculates the HDI to distinguish between regions, genders, and ethnic groups, thus avoiding 'broad brush' conclusions to be drawn based on aggregates.	The HDI may overstate development in countries with high inequality (e.g. Latin American countries) as aggregates mask the low quality of life endured by a large number.

In 2010 David Cameron asked the Office of National Statistics (ONS) to devise a new measure of well-being.

> "From April next year we will start measuring our progress as a country not just by how our economy is growing, but by how our lives are improving; not just by our standard of living, but by our quality of life."
>
> **David Cameron**, *Prime Minister, speech on 25th October 2010.*[1]

Beginning in April 2011, the ONS now collect **subjective** well-being estimates to complement existing socio-economic indicators to allow a fuller statistical picture of the nation's well-being. A large sample size is taken which allows for comparisons to be made across regions, genders and ethnic groups. The subjective questions asked are:

● Overall, how satisfied are you with your life nowadays?

● Overall, to what extent do you feel the things you do in your life are worthwhile?

● Overall, how happy did you feel yesterday?

● Overall, how anxious did you feel yesterday?

The first results of this survey published in April 2012 were considered by the ONS to be 'experimental', but they had some interesting findings. Women scored more highly than men on the life satisfaction and worthwhile ratings, but scored lower on the anxiety question. Younger and older people scored more highly on the life satisfaction, worthwhile, happiness and anxiety ratings whereas middle aged people tended to score lower in all of these. Overall reported personal well-being has improved every year since financial year ending 2012 when data were first collected, suggesting that an increasing number of people in the UK are feeling positive about their lives.

Question

1. The UK experienced unbroken growth from 1992 to 2008. To what extent has this resulted in a higher quality of life for UK citizens?

We turn next to the subject of inequality in incomes.

● ● Knowledge and Application: Measuring UK income inequality

Figure 4.3: Weekly UK net household income at each percentile point in 2014-15

Source: Belfield, Cribb, Hood & Joyce, *Living Standards, Inequality and Poverty in the UK 2016*, IFS

Before looking at changes in the distribution of income in recent years, let's take a look at how income is distributed across UK households in absolute terms.

As we can see from Figure 4.3, household incomes at the median level are almost double those at the 10th percentile, and incomes at the 90th percentile are just over double those at the median. At the top of the distribution there is significant income inequality, with income at the 99th percentile being around £2,400 per week, over two-and-a-half times the income of the 90th percentile.

1. David Cameron, speech on 25th October 2010, http://www.number10.gov.uk/news/britain's-wellbeing-to-be-measured/

Figure 4.4: Mean equivalised household disposable income (£) 1977-2014

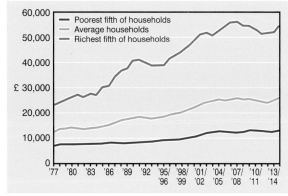

Source: ONS

Changes in income inequality can be measured by looking at changes in the income of **quintile groups**. The lowest quintile group represents changes in the income of the poorest 20% of households, while the top quintile represents changes in the income of the richest 20% of households. From Figure 4.4 we can clearly see that inequality increased dramatically under the Conservative government of 1979-1997, with the top quintile seeing a much larger rise in income than the bottom quintile. Under the Labour government from 1997-2010 growth in overall inequality was slowed, and then reversed slightly under the Coalition government of 2010-15.

Using quintiles to look at changes in income inequality has its limitations. It hides changes in incomes within quintiles by aggregating them.

During the Great Recession of 2008-09 and the stalling recovery of 2010-12, the fortunes of those at the top have declined in absolute and relative terms. As previously mentioned average real disposable household incomes started falling after the end of the recession in 2009. As shown by Figure 4.5, the incomes of the richest households have been hit harder than the incomes of the poorest households. Between 2007 and 2013, the real incomes of the richest households fell by over 8%, while those in the bottom 20% experienced some low growth in their real incomes, thus causing a fall in the level of income inequality. One

Figure 4.5: Real income growth by percentile point, 2007–08 to 2014–15 (UK)

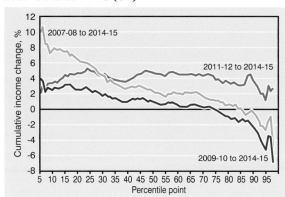

Source: Belfield, Cribb, Hood & Joyce, *Living Standards, Inequality and Poverty in the UK 2016*, IFS

to the biggest reasons for inequality falling over this period is that benefit payments, including pensions, remained relatively stable or rose while real household earnings from work fell. However, the 2011-12 to 2014-15 line shows that inequality changed very little during the most recent years from the data, as real earnings growth took hold when growth strengthened and inflation tumbled from 2012, and planned welfare reforms such as benefit cuts were carried out. This somewhat slowed the trend of falling inequality seen over the 5 years from 2007-08 to 2012-13.

Question

2. How might economists compare income inequality **between** countries?

● ● Application **and** Analysis: **The Gini coefficient system**

The Gini coefficient is a commonly used statistical measure of income inequality. The Gini coefficient gives a number between 0 and 1, where 0 represents prefect equality, and 1 represents perfect inequality (all the income goes to one household). The decimal can also be expressed as a percentage. The measure takes into account all of the income distribution.

Figure 4.6: The Gini coefficient (%) equivalised disposable income 1977 to 2014/15

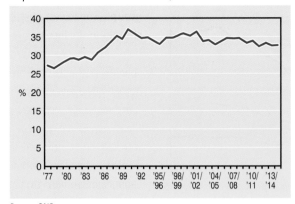

Source: ONS

Figure 4.7: 90/10 ratio and share of national income going to the top 1%

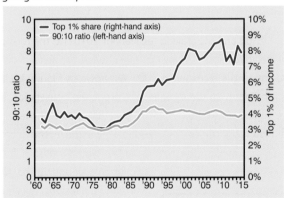

Source: Belfield, Cribb, Hood & Joyce, *Living Standards, Inequality and Poverty in the UK 2016*, IFS

Figure 4.8: 80/20 ratio, 1977 to 2014/15

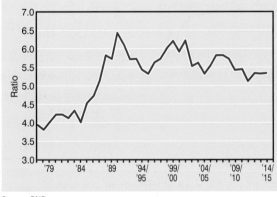

Source: ONS

Another common measure of inequality is the ratio of the income of one particular percentile to another. It is simply the ratio of household income at a certain percentile expressed as a ratio of the household income of a selected lower percentile. This measure is particularly useful because it compares just two points in the distribution, whereas the gini co-efficient takes the whole distribution into account, and so can be distorted by significant changes at the extremes. As can be seen from Figure 4.7, although there was a broad-based rise in inequality between percentiles in the 1980s, income inequality between most households has remained fairly stable since the early 1990s according to the 90:10 ratio, and shows some decline in inequality from the early 1990s to 2015. The 80:20 ratio in Figure 4.8 also shows declining income inequality after 2000. However, the very top households have pulled away significantly, even from relatively well-off households. Figure 4.7 shows that the share of total income that goes to the top 1% of households has risen from 3% in 1979 to 8% in 2015.

As can be seen from Figure 4.7, although there was a broad-based rise in inequality between percentiles in the 1980s, income inequality between most households has remained fairly stable since the early 1990s. The 90:10 ratio shows the ratio of the average income of a household in the 90th percentile to that of the average household in the 10th percentile. If the 90:10 ratio is 4, this means that on average, households in the 90th percentile have four times as much income as households in the 10th percentile. The 90:10 ratio actually shows some decline in inequality from the early 1990s to 2015. The 80:20 ratio in Figure 4.8 also shows declining income inequality after 2000.

● ● Application and Analysis: Recent trends in income inequality and their causes

Trying to get a comprehensive picture about trends in income inequality is difficult and this is why it is important to look at a number of measures as data on **overall** income inequality can mask changes **within** the income distribution. Given the data above, there are a number of conclusions that we can draw about income inequality in the UK. The causes of these changes are also explained.

1979-1990: Rising inequality

It is clear from all measures that there was a rapid and widespread increase in income inequality during the 1980s. The Gini coefficient rose from 0.26 to 0.34 during the decade, and Figure 4.7 shows that under the Conservative governments of 1979-1997 the higher the level of income, the higher the rate of income growth.

There are several underlying reasons for the rapid rise in inequality during this period:

1. *Technology and demand for skills* – Earnings (or 'original income') inequality grew rapidly. Technological change reduced demand for low skilled workers in a number of industries (e.g. computers can do much of the work of clerks). At the same time, advanced technology has made skilled workers who can effectively use the new technology more productive, thus raising their reward through higher wages (e.g. accountants can use computer programmes to raise their output).

2. *Rapid deindustrialisation* through removing state support for heavy industry reduced the demand for lots of workers in these industries. Structural unemployment affected many, and male participation in the workforce declined, reducing the incomes of these households.

3. The 1980s saw a rapid rise in *female participation* in the workforce. This led to a widening gap between no-earner and two-earner households.

4. Spurred on by government initiatives to encourage entrepreneurship, the number of *self-employed workers grew rapidly*. As the variation in the earnings of self-employed workers is higher than for all workers, earnings inequality grew overall.

5. In 1981 *state benefits became linked to inflation rather than earnings*. As earnings tend to rise more quickly than prices those on benefits saw their incomes fall behind the incomes of those in work.

6. Government policies to *reduce the power of trade unions* meant less wage bargaining power for (usually) relatively low paid workers in many industries.

7. Dramatic *cuts in top rates of income tax* increased the disposable incomes of those at the top, while the switch to a *greater level of indirect taxation* significantly reduced the real incomes of those with lower incomes, thus widening inequality.

1990-97: Stable, slightly falling inequality

From 1990 to 1997 inequality remained historically high but fell very slightly overall, as shown by the Gini coefficient in Figure 4.6. There are a number of reasons for this:

1. The rapid economic growth of the mid to late 1980s which caused the earnings of those at the top to pull away from the rest was not prevalent during this period. The early 90s recession and aftermath caused the incomes of higher earners to suffer, as shown by the significant fall in the share of income going to the top 1% from 1992 to 1995 in Figure 4.7.

2. Direct taxation was increased in the early 1990s, hitting the richest the hardest.

3. Means-tested benefits were introduced in the early 1990s, giving more help to low earners who were in true need of financial help.

1997-2004/5: Generally stable overall inequality, convergence for most, divergence at the top and bottom

Under Labour, from 1997 to 2004-05 the overall level of inequality remained roughly stable, fluctuating between 0.34 and 0.35. However, the most notable changes during this period were changes within the income distribution. Figure 4.7 shows that the share of income taken by the top 1% of households grew much quicker in this period than the income of other households during this period. However, the 90/10 ratio shows that the income gap between the 90th and 10th percentiles remained fairly constant. At the same time, under Labour the bottom percentile were the only group who saw their real disposable income actually fall. So, the gap between the 'haves' and 'have nots' certainly did increase between 1997 and 2004-05, due to rapidly rising real incomes at the top and falling real incomes at the bottom. Excluding the top and bottom deciles however, income inequality actually fell slightly, as shown by the 80/20 and 90/10 ratios. There are several reasons why these changes occurred:

1. The *process of globalisation* was rapid and powerful during this period. As UK companies expanded their operations to overseas markets, the actions of top managers could, arguably, raise the value they added to their companies, and thus higher salaries could be justified. Furthermore, in a more globalised economy demand for highly skilled labour including top managers, architects, engineers etc. is very high (just think about the demand for these workers in places like Dubai and Kuwait), thus the salaries of highly-skilled labour grew.

2. The New Labour government cracked down on workers claiming benefits, and incapacity benefit in particular, by *tightening the eligibility criteria for benefits*. In addition the government clamped down on those claiming benefits that they deemed to be capable of work. This caused the income of some at the bottom of the distribution to fall.

3. *Public sector employment* grew dramatically under New Labour (by around 850,000). *Pay awards* for public sector workers *exceeded inflation* during this period, and thus the real incomes of a growing number of public sector workers increased considerably, helping many in low paid public sector jobs to catch up with median household income.

4. One of the first pieces of legislation passed by the Labour government was the introduction of the *national minimum wage*. The minimum wage increased faster than the rate of inflation during this period, thus boosting the real incomes of those in work on low pay, helping to close the gap to median earnings.

5. The introduction of *tax credits* for working families on low income helped to increase the real disposable incomes of many households.

6. During this period *unemployment fell* considerably, from 2.18 million at the beginning of 1997 to 1.43 million at the beginning of 2005. This fall meant that many at the lower end of the income distribution saw their incomes grow as they gained employment.

7. *National Insurance Contributions* (*NICs*), which are broadly progressive, increased from 2003 which reduced the inequality of disposable household incomes.

2004/5 – 2008/9: Rising income inequality

From 2004-05 to 2008-09 there was a general rise in income inequality, with the Gini coefficient, 90/10 and 80/20 ratios all increasing. This suggests a significant increase in inequality spread across the distribution, although high earners saw particularly strong income growth during this period. This rise in inequality occurred due to:

1. From mid-2005 *unemployment started to rise*, causing a fall in the incomes of those who lost their jobs.

2. From 2004-05 until the beginning of 2008 *share prices and company profits* were rising considerably. Therefore bankers, financial traders and company bosses increased their pay packets (including bonuses) in line with this, raising incomes at the top end.

3. In 2004 the *EU expanded* to include 10 new member states from Central and Eastern Europe. The UK was one of just 3 of the existing EU members who allowed open access to their labour market for migrant workers from the accession states. The UK government estimated that around 40,000 migrants would come to the UK from the new EU members, but by the end of the decade around 1 million had arrived. The productive migrant workers were willing to work for relatively little pay, putting downward pressure on wages in mostly unskilled, low paid jobs. Although this helped to control wage inflation in the economy, it hindered the wage growth of relatively unskilled workers in the UK.

2008/09 – 2016: A dramatic fall in income inequality or a one off?

From 2008-09 to 2012-13 a mixed picture emerges. Figures 4.7 and 4.8 show that the 90/10 and 80/20 ratios all fell from 2008-09. In addition, Figure 4.5 shows that during the troubled years of 2007-08 to

2012-13 higher income groups saw significantly larger falls in real income than any other group, with a fall of over 8% for the highest percentile, while the lowest percentile groups saw small increases in their real income. All this suggests a fall in income inequality.

There are several reasons for these changes:

1. The rapid rise in the income of those at the top of the distribution between 2008-09 to 2009-10 was due to high earners bringing income forward (known as *'forestalling'*) in order to *avoid the new 50% income tax rate on income* above £150,000 which was introduced by the Labour government and came into effect in April 2010. This meant that although incomes at the top end grew dramatically from 2008-09 to 2009-10, they then fell considerably from 2009-10, causing the Gini coefficient to fall by some way.

2. Real disposable incomes at the bottom rose significantly from 2008-09 to 2010-11 due to rises in tax credits and state benefits higher than the rate of inflation, which fell dramatically due to the recession. As earnings growth from 2009 onwards was extremely low, and negative in real terms for many, out of work benefits increased at a faster rate than earnings, causing a fall in real income inequality.

3. Despite the effects of forestalling in 2009-10, the incomes of those at the top have been hit the hardest by the Great Recession and its aftermath. As shown in Figure 4.5: the higher the level of income, the greater the fall in real incomes from 2007 to 2013. Some estimates suggest that the real incomes of the top 1% have fallen by 15% since the full effects of the financial crisis were felt. The UK economy has a very large financial services sector (roughly 10% of GDP), and workers in this sector tend to have high pay. In the aftermath of the financial crisis employment in the City of London has fell by 7%, which has put downward pressure on pay in the sector. In addition poor macroeconomic conditions from 2008 to 2013 have meant that there is less justification for large bonuses in the financial sector and in the board room as share prices and company profits have struggled. Also, negative media attention and public opinion over 'excessive' executive pay has constrained the pay of top earners. Shareholder revolts have also put the brakes on boardroom pay.

4. Very strong employment growth from 2013 to 2016 helped to reduce income inequality. Despite the fact that many of the jobs created were not full time and often low paid service sector jobs, employment rose by 500,000 from 2014-15 to 2015-16 causing average earnings to rise by 2.4%. This caused overall inequality to fall despite the fact that most working age benefits only rose by 1%.

Perhaps the most notable point to make is not the changes in UK income inequality that have occurred in the last decade, but the **level** of income inequality which is very high by historical standards, and high compared to most other advanced European economies. Many of the underlying causes of rising inequality in the 1980s are still prevalent as reasons for higher levels of inequality in the UK today, and earnings or 'original' income inequality remains high as the labour market rewards highly skilled workers much more than those with few skills. So, despite the fall in income inequality following the Great Recession, historically high income inequality is likely to last into the long term, as the underlying causes of high inequality remain.

● Knowledge: **The case for and against inequality**

Free market economists argue that inequality is necessary for the efficient functioning of the economy. Workers are paid according to their productivity, and therefore this creates the incentive for workers to work hard. Without the rewards of higher earnings workers would be less productive, and the threat of economic hardship for those who don't work hard makes the economy more productive, encouraging growth and efficiency. Furthermore, free market economists say that inequality is justified as different workers add different levels of value to their employer. If a good CEO performs well and makes decisions which add an extra £300 million to their company's revenue, then it is justified for them to be paid more than a secretary at the same company as their value added is considerably less.

Critics of this free market approach argue that inequality is not justified as all workers are part of the wealth creation process, not just the entrepreneurial class. Furthermore, in their book *The Spirit Level* which attracted a great deal of attention Wilkinson and Pickett provide evidence to suggest that societies with greater levels of inequality suffer from resultant negative externalities such as higher levels of crime, worse public health, and lower social cohesion. In 2014 the Equality Trust thinktank estimated that the cost of inequality, through its impact on health, wellbeing and crime rates, to be £39bn per year. In addition to the external costs of inequality, there is the argument that people on lower incomes spend a higher proportion of their income. Redistribution from higher to lower income groups will therefore increase overall consumption and output.

Question

3. Income inequality has been in the spotlight since the 2008 financial crisis and the subsequent recession. To what extent is the UK's current level of inequality damaging for growth and overall social welfare?

There is clear evidence that the overall level of inequality in the UK has not fallen significantly since 1997 despite efforts by the Labour and Coalition governments to redistribute income. The tax and benefit system is redistributive by nature. The incomes of the richest after taxes and benefits are lower than before, and the incomes of the poorest after taxes and benefits are higher.

Table 4.2: The effects of taxes and benefits on household income

Original income (wages, salaries, self-employment income, pensions, investment income)		
add	Cash Benefits	= **Gross income**
subtract	Direct taxes and NICs	= **Disposable income**
subtract	Indirect taxes	= **Post tax income**
add	Benefits in kind (e.g. NHS)	= **Final income**

In 2010/11 the top quintile of households had an average original income 16 times greater than the bottom quintile (£81,500 compared to £5,100). After taxes and benefits the average income of the top quintile was just four times greater than that of the bottom quintile (£61,400 compared to £15,200).

Figure 4.9 shows that direct taxes and cash benefits redistribute income. If you take original income (income before any taxes or benefits), and add cash benefits, this gives gross income. As cash benefits boost the incomes of poorer households far more than richer households, income inequality falls substantially as shown by the fact that the gini co-efficient is far lower for gross income than for original income. Once direct taxes are subtracted from gross income, this gives disposable income. As richer households pay a higher proportion of their income in direct taxes than poorer households, income inequality falls, as shown by the fact that the gini co-efficient for disposable income is lower than for gross income. However, the fall in the gini coefficient in the shift from gross to disposable income is less than it is from original to gross income, meaning that cash benefits have a more redistributive effect than direct taxes. Figure 4.10 shows how direct taxes and cash benefits affect the relative position of different income groups. The net effect is to boost the incomes of lower income groups, and reduce the incomes of higher income groups.

Figure 4.9: Gini coefficients for original, gross and disposable income, 1977 to 2014/15

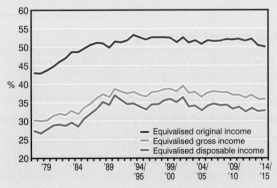

Source: ONS

Figure 4.10: Summary of the effects of direct taxes and cash benefits on all households, 2014/15

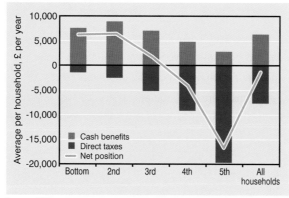

Source: ONS

Direct taxes are taxes which are levied directly on an individual or organisation e.g. income tax. Most direct taxes are **progressive**, meaning that the higher the level of income the greater the proportion of income is taken in tax. Indirect taxes are taxes paid on expenditure on goods and services e.g. VAT, tobacco duty. Indirect taxes are **regressive**, meaning that the higher the level of income the lower the proportion of income is taken in tax. The tax system in the UK overall does little to redistribute income. The benefit system is far more redistributive. Although some cash benefits are **universal** such as the state pension, many are **means-tested** such as income support, and as of 2013, child benefit, which had previously been universal. The change was made as part of the government's deficit reduction strategy.

●● Analysis and Evaluation: Government policies to tackle inequality and work poverty

Several policies have been introduced to address inequality and we summarise the key measures.

● The **National Minimum Wage** (**NMW**) – came into effect in 1999 and since then the government has increased the NMW faster than the rates of both inflation and earnings in most years. As of 1st October 2016 the rate for workers aged 21-24 and over stood at £6.95, while it was at £5.55 for 18-20 year olds and £4.00 for those under 18. Supporters of the NMW claim that it reduces poverty and worker exploitation. At the same time it provides a strong incentive for people to work, thus reducing the unemployment and poverty traps. From 1 April 2016, the government introduced a new mandatory **national living wage** (**NLW**) for workers **aged 25 and above**, initially set at £7.20.

The NMW has its critics from the right and left of the political spectrum. Some critics of the NMW say that despite large and growing differences in living costs between regions, there is no regional variation in the NMW. In London where the cost of living is highest there has been a campaign for employers to adopt a London 'Living Wage' which stood at £9.75 per hour in 2016. The Living Wage Foundation says this is the lowest wage that allows people to meet the cost of living, and was set at £8.45 for the rest of the UK in 2016. The Living Wage has been supported by all of the main political parties but it is voluntary, and not legally binding, though the lower, National Living Wage, is legally binding. Critics also point out that although the NMW did not appear to cause unemployment during the NICE decade, during the subsequent recession, when businesses were less willing to hire workers the NMW could have had a negative impact on employment. Some think tanks warned that the introduction of the NLW would cost an estimated 60,000 jobs, but since its introduction there is no clear evidence that employment has suffered as a result.

● The **Working and Children's Tax Credits** – both came into effect in April 2003 to divide the old Working Families Tax Credit into two parts.

The Child Tax Credit can be claimed by people who are responsible for children regardless of whether they are in or out of work. Households on lower income receive a greater amount through the Child Tax Credit system.

The main aim of the Working Tax Credit is to 'make work pay'. Those on low incomes with or without children are able to claim this tax credit. The scheme is designed to improve the incentive to work, thus increasing participation rates and reducing the **poverty trap**. The poverty trap is where a worker, often working part time, has no incentive to work harder or for longer, as this would result in benefits being lost (e.g. free school meals for children) and a greater amount being taken in tax. Thus, the very high effective marginal tax rate discourages work. The Working Tax Credit also reduces the **unemployment trap** by increasing the rewards from work over the income from benefits.

However, the tax credit system is not without its criticisms:

- There will always be a 'withdrawal zone', where benefits are being removed as incomes rise. The existence of this zone provides less of an incentive to work more hours, or take better jobs.
- Tax credits cost the Treasury around £25bn per annum, an enormous cost.
- The system is very complex, and thus there is a large administrative cost associated with the level of bureaucracy. Furthermore, many applying for tax credits complain about the difficulty of the forms that need to be filled in. This complexity has caused the 'take-up rate' for the Working Tax Credit in particular, to be low, at just 61% in 2009/10 according to the HMRC. Furthermore, the complex nature of the system has led to administrative mistakes, with the HMRC overpaying claimants by some £6bn between 2003 and 2007. Fraud has also been a serious problem.

- The **introduction of the 50% top rate of income tax** – in April 2010 a new 50% top rate of income tax was introduced on incomes above £150,000. The Chancellor Alistair Darling introduced the top rate as an 'emergency measure' in his April 2009 budget. It was intended to raise £6bn in tax revenue, as well as reducing income inequality. However, the HMRC estimate that it has raised very little, and Chancellor George Osborne announced in his March 2012 budget that the top rate of income tax would be cut to 45% in April 2013, where it has remained.

- **The New Deal (known as the 'Flexible New Deal' from 2009)** – this programme is aimed at providing training, subsidised employment and voluntary work for the unemployed, thus providing them with the skills necessary to obtain a job. Furthermore, the New Deal introduced the ability to withdraw benefits from those who refused 'reasonable employment'.

- **Government funding of apprenticeships** – there has been widespread cross-party support for greater funding of apprenticeships which are seen as a good way of providing people with the skills employers demand and reducing skills shortages in various sectors. However, four out of five companies claim they face barriers to hiring apprentices such as administrative issues and employer's liability insurance.

- **Improving 'in kind' benefits** – the funding of education and healthcare has increased considerably since 1997. Better education and healthcare should help the poorest proportionally more, as it means they should have the level of health and skills that are necessary to be rewarded in the labour market, thus reducing inter-generational poverty.

- **Cutting the basic rate of income tax** – in 2007 the Chancellor Gordon Brown cut the basic rate of income tax from 22% to 20%, claiming that this would increase the disposable incomes of many low income families. However, to fund this, he scrapped the lower 10% rate, meaning that many of the poorest families actually saw a fall in their overall disposable incomes. This drew sharp criticism and the government extended tax credits to try to offset the effects of the tax change.

- **Increasing the tax free personal allowance** – one of the main redistributive policies of the Coalition government was to raise the personal allowance (how much taxable income you can have before you start paying Income Tax) from £6,475 in 2009-10 to £10,000 in 2014-15. This was a key feature of the Liberal Democrat election manifesto in 2010. By 2016-17 it had been raised to £11,000. This has partly been funded by meagre increases in the higher 40% tax threshold, with rises in the threshold falling well behind inflation, causing what's known as 'fiscal drag'. Following the 2014-15 budget it has been estimated that 1.1m more people pay some of their income at the higher 40% tax rate than would have under Labour's published plans in 2010. As a result of these changes, lower income households are better off overall, while higher income households pay a higher proportion of their income in tax.

- **The Winter Fuel Payment and fuel poverty** – the allowance, first introduced in the winter of 1997/98 was aimed at reducing the level fuel poverty amongst the elderly. Since then however, the payment has been made universal in the sense that it can be claimed by any household with a member over the age of 60. Critics say the measure is very costly for the Treasury, and poorly targeted.

Despite these measures, there has been widespread concern that the policy adopted by both the Coalition (2010-2015) and the Conservative (elected in 2015) governments of favouring spending cuts over tax increases to reduce the budget deficit will affect poorer, more vulnerable households the most, as public services and benefit payments are continually squeezed.

● ● Knowledge and Application: The distribution of wealth in the UK

Unlike income which is a flow, wealth is a **stock** concept. Household wealth is the total value of assets owned by the household at a point in time. Marketable wealth incorporates physical wealth such as houses, land and cars, as well as financial wealth such as financial assets like shares and bonds. Non-marketable wealth (wealth that cannot be sold to anyone else) mainly consists of pension rights. Wealth is usually more unevenly distributed than income, as it is accumulated over a lifetime. Those on higher incomes are able to accumulate wealth through savings, buying shares, getting a mortgage to purchase a house etc. whereas those on lower incomes will struggle to do this. Those with high educational attainment tend to be rewarded in the labour market, and thus wealth and educational achievement are positively correlated. In addition, wealth increases with age, as it is accumulated during one's working life. Since wealth generates income (e.g. shares pay dividends) wealth inequality is a significant cause of income inequality. Average household wealth has increased considerably over the past 25 years, more than doubling between 1987 and 2009, increasing from £56,000 to £117,000 (at 2008-09 prices). Household wealth has fallen slightly after 2007 mostly due to a fall in property prices but increases in house prices from 2013 onwards has reversed this.

Wealth is far more unequally distributed than is income. According to IFS data, the Gini coefficient is 0.64 for wealth, compared to 0.34 for net income. The wealthiest 1% of households hold about 20% of household wealth, the top 5% hold approximately 40%, and the top 10% hold over 50% of wealth. Meanwhile, Figure 4.11 shows that the poorest households struggle to accumulate any wealth at all. This is because the marginal propensity to save is very low for low income households as a high proportion of income must be spent to afford basic necessities. Low income households therefore struggle to build up share portfolios, deposits to buy houses and other sources of wealth.

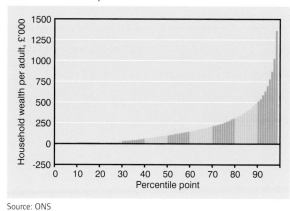

Figure 4.11: Distribution (by percentile) of total household wealth per adult

Source: ONS

Extension material: the inheritance tax debate

Inheritance tax is a hotly debated topic. Inheritance tax is levied at 40% on wealth valued at more than £325,000 (in 2014/15) unless it is left to your spouse. The threshold for married couples and civil partners is £650,000. One of the Conservatives' key manifesto promises for the 2010 election was to raise the inheritance tax threshold to £1 million. They claimed that passing on your wealth to family members when you die was a natural instinct, and people should have the right to do so. Others, such as the American billionaire investor Warren Buffet are staunch supporters of high inheritance tax. They argue that inheritance tax is one of the few progressive taxes remaining, and it reduces intergenerational wealth and income inequality. Furthermore, allowing people to inherit large amounts of wealth from their parents discourages work and entrepreneurial activity, and some argue that their high standard of living isn't 'earned'. Buffet has warned that the US is in danger of creating an 'oligarchy' if inheritance tax isn't increased. When the Coalition government was formed in 2010 the Liberal Democrats had their preferred policy implemented of raising the personal allowance on income tax, and the inheritance tax threshold was not raised significantly.

● Knowledge: **Poverty definitions**

It is hard to say what exactly 'poverty' means, as people's interpretations as to what constitutes poverty are different. However, economists split poverty into two categories.

Absolute poverty is the situation where an individual, household or group struggle to obtain the basic necessities required to sustain human life such as food, water, and clean clothes.

Relative poverty is the situation in which an individual, household or group faces a low material standard of living relative to the rest of society, and are in danger of **social exclusion**. In the UK members of a household are in relative poverty if their household income is less than 60% of the median. This is known as the 'poverty line'.

● ● Application and Analysis: **Changes in poverty since 1997**

As income inequality increased between 1979 and 1990 the number of households in relative poverty rose significantly, with child poverty increasing three fold during this period. Although the early and mid-1990s saw a stabilising or even a slight reversal in child poverty rates, by 1997, the UK's child poverty rate was amongst the worst of all rich nations with around one in three children living in relative poverty. When Labour came to power in 1997 they made a concrete pledge to reduce poverty rates, with a particular focus on child poverty. During Labour's first two terms (1997-2005) policies such as the introduction of the Working Families Tax Credit, the Child Tax Credit, and more generous means-tested benefits for pensioners

Figure 4.12: Percentage of people living in relative poverty in the UK, 1999-2014

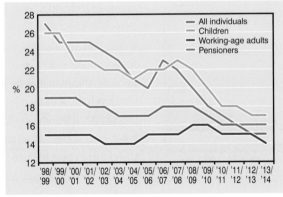

Source: ONS

contributed to a fall in poverty rates for all groups as shown in Figure 4.12. However, during Labour's third term child and overall poverty rates rose until the onset of the Great Recession. Since the recession of 2008-09 the overall relative poverty rate has fallen slightly. However, this masks the changes in the absolute living standards of the poorest as the real incomes of households around the poverty line are roughly the same as they were 10 years ago, and once housing costs are considered, poverty rates were the same at the start of 2017 as in 2007. This shows how housing costs adversely affect poverty.

● ● Analysis and Evaluation: **Influences on Relative Poverty and the limitations of the measure**

Influences on Poverty Rates 1997-2007

The Labour government was unsuccessful in meeting overall and child poverty reduction targets despite increasing average spending per child in the social security system. One of the main reasons poverty reduction did not occur is due to the problem with the relative poverty measure. Despite adopting poverty reduction targets the New Labour government had a very relaxed stance on general levels of inequality, and particularly rapid income growth at the top of the income distribution. Given that the relative poverty line is measured by 60% of median household income, the only way poverty rates can fall is if incomes at the bottom of the distribution grow quicker than those in the middle. Another contributing factor was the system of state benefits being linked to inflation, which was lower than earnings growth throughout the vast majority of Labour's time in office. Therefore, despite rises in absolute living standards for many of those at the bottom end of the income distribution, relative poverty rates remained stubbornly high.

Downward pressure on poverty rates 2007-2017

The effects of the 2008-09 recession and subsequent squeeze on household incomes caused a fall in relative poverty rates. This may seem counter-intuitive at first. As previously mentioned, since the Great Recession the incomes of those at the bottom of the distribution have been squeezed by less than those at top and the middle of the distribution as shown in Figure 4.5. Therefore, despite falling real incomes across the board, the incomes of the poorest have caught up with the median, thus causing relative poverty rates to fall. So despite falling living standards at the bottom end of the distribution in the aftermath of the Great Recession, relative poverty rates have fallen. This highlights a key problem with the measure; it tells us little about absolute living standards.

Between 2007 and 2010 earnings growth was very weak. The public sector in the UK employs around one quarter of all those employed and the public sector pay freeze, followed by subsequent increases of just 1% per year, meant that earnings grew very slowly during this period in the public sector, and high unemployment meant that private sector pay growth was also anaemic. Benefits, on the other hand, were linked to inflation, which was, on average, much higher during this period, as shown in Figure 4.13. This bolstered the relative income position of the poorest, which puts significant downward pressure on poverty rates.

Another factor which has caused poverty rates to fall is the decline in household worklessness. The falls in worklessness seen in recent years were the continuation of a much longer-run trend: the proportion of children living in a workless household fell from 23% in 1993–94 to 13% in 2014–15. This is explained in part by policies designed to encourage parental employment, and in particular lone-parent employment. However, two-thirds of children in income poverty already live in a working household, meaning that in future, further declines in worklessness will do little to reduce poverty rates, and the relative earnings of low income households will matter far more in determining overall poverty rates.

Upward pressure on poverty rates 2007-2017

The biggest upward pressure on income poverty rates has been the falls in real earnings from 2008 to 2014. Figure 4.13 shows that during this period prices were growing more rapidly than average earnings, thereby reducing real incomes. Increases in housing costs, primarily above inflation rent rises during this period also had an impact on poverty rates, but this effect was relatively small.

Another limitation of the relative poverty measure is that it does little to inform us about the living standards of those who are in poverty, and whether their absolute living standards are improving or not. There is some evidence to suggest that the hardship of those in poverty is growing. Despite a general fall in relative poverty since 1997, relative poverty using a threshold of 40% of median income has risen, showing a rise in the proportion of the population who are 'very poor'. In addition, income is not the only thing that affects the material living standards of those in poverty. Factors such as household indebtedness, for example, have a big impact on the living standards and anxiety levels of the poorest in society. 'Pay Day Lending' increased markedly in the wake of the 2008 financial crisis, as mainstream banks became increasingly unwilling to engage in unsecured

Figure 4.13: Annual growth in average regular weekly pay over the three months to the stated month (seasonally adjusted) (%) and annual growth rate for the CPI inflation (%)

Source: ONS

lending to groups with a high risk of default. Thus, the financial position of many poor households declined, and food banks became increasingly common in the UK.

As many planned benefit cuts come into full effect the absolute living standards for those at the bottom end of the distribution may well fall. Whether relative poverty rates rise or not depends on how the incomes of other groups alter in coming years.

Question

4. Evaluate the effectiveness of three policies which might be used to reduce inequality and eradicate poverty.

● Evaluation: Persistent poverty

An interesting perspective on poverty is to look at how long households spend in poverty. **Persistent poverty** is defined as experiencing relative poverty (household income less than 60% of median) in the current year, as well as at least 2 out of the 3 preceding years. In 2014, 6.5% of the UK population were in persistent poverty, equivalent to approximately 3.9 million people. The UK has the third-lowest persistent poverty rate in the EU, but the overall poverty rate for 2014, at 16.8%, was the 12th highest.

Figure 4.14 shows overall poverty in the UK compared with other EU countries. It shows that the UK compares particularly well on a measure of persistent poverty compared to other EU member states. Poverty in the UK is more transient than in other EU economies, and although lone-parent and pensioner households in particular struggle, it is easier for UK households to leave poverty than in other European countries such as Lithuania or Spain. The main reason for this is that unemployment is relatively low, and job creation is relatively high, meaning that households in the UK have a greater chance of accessing employment, thereby boosting household income.

Figure 4.14: Persistent and overall poverty rates, UK and EU average, 2008 to 2014, percentage total population

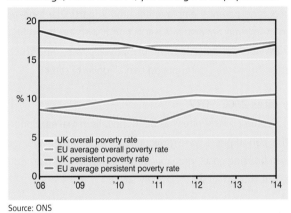

Source: ONS

●● Knowledge and Application: An economic divide between regions

Overall data on inequality and poverty in the UK hides substantial inequality between regions. Historically Regional Policy has been used to help support less prosperous regions but over time the UK has had to adopt a more 'hands off' approach to comply with EU Regional Policy framework and its strong opposition to 'unfair' competition such as state aid. Two remaining initiatives with regional dimensions include:

● The Selective Finance for Investment in England and Scotland program – offers grants to support start-ups, business expansion, innovation and R&D.

● The European Regional Development Fund.

Figure 4.15 shows the considerable variation in weekly earnings between regions, with weekly earnings in London being 35% higher than those in the North East. Also, the data shows something of a North-South divide. The only three regions whose median weekly earnings exceeded that of the UK average were London, East of England and the South-East.

Figure 4.15: Median full-time gross weekly earnings (£), April 2016

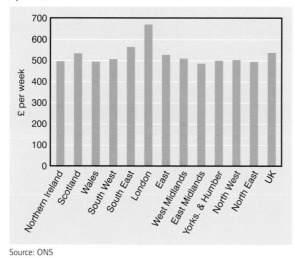

Source: ONS

Figure 4.16: Average house price by country and region April 2004 to April 2016

Source: ONS

Between 2000 and 2007 many of the less prosperous regions such as the North East started to close the gap as they experienced significant falls in unemployment and rises in house prices. During and after the 2008-09 recession however, Northern Regions suffered more from rising unemployment and house price falls, while property in London and the South-East maintained value better. Furthermore, the local economies of several 'outer' regions such as the North-East and Wales have become very dependent upon the public sector. The Coalition's spending and public sector jobs cuts (amounting to 180,000 between 2010 and 2013) have hit those regions the hardest, and the North-South divide appears to be getting larger once again.

Figures 4.15 and 4.16 show much higher levels of earnings and house prices are in London than other regions. This has led some economists to point to a London – other regions divide, rather than a North – South divide. However, the London economy is not without its problems. As shown in Table 4.3 unemployment and inactivity rates are above the national average. High house prices have made many dependent upon housing benefit. Obtaining work or more work would mean this important source of income would be lost, creating a large disincentive. Furthermore, the absence of a London minimum wage further reduces the incentive to work. Child poverty is also a major problem in London. The campaign group End Child Poverty estimate that 1 in 4 children in London live in poverty, compared to 1 in 5 nationally. The London borough of Tower Hamlets has the highest child poverty level in the UK, at 52%. This highlights a key point of note; there is as much of a divide *within* regions as there is *between* regions.

Table 4.3: Unemployment and inactivity rates by region, seasonally adjusted, February to April 2016

	Unemployment rate (%)	Inactivity rates (%)		Unemployment rate (%)	Inactivity rates (%)
United Kingdom	5.0	21.8	East Midlands	4.5	21.6
Wales	4.8	24.3	West Midlands	5.7	24.1
Scotland	5.8	22.2	East	3.7	19.2
Northern Ireland	5.8	26.0	London	5.9	22.0
North East	7.3	23.9	South East	3.9	18.7
North West	4.9	23.3	South West	4.1	19.3
Yorks and Humber	5.9	23.0			

Source: ONS

Chapter 5
UK Trade, the Current Account and the Value of the Pound

This chapter examines the position of, and recent changes in, the different components of the current account on balance of payments. The significance of the UK's persistent current account deficit is then discussed. Finally, the chapter identifies recent changes in the external value of the pound sterling, the causes of these changes and their importance.

● Knowledge: **The meaning of the current account**

There are three components of the Balance of Payments: The Current Account, the Financial Account and the Capital Account. The most important component of which is the current account balance, which this chapter will focus upon.

In short, the current account measures flows of income into and out of the economy. Each section is itself a 'balance', i.e. it takes into account both inflows and outflows. The current account contains four sections:

1. The **balance of trade in goods**: such as automobiles, pharmaceuticals, agricultural products and oil, calculated by value of exported goods minus value of goods imported.

2. The **balance of trade in services**: such as financial services, shipping and tourism, calculated by value of exported services minus value of services imported.

3. The **primary income balance**, also known as *net investment income balance*, or *income balance* is the balance of factor income i.e. net income from employing factors of production. This could include interest from loans made, dividends from shares purchased, profits from a company's operations, or remittances sent to family members. So, if a UK company makes a profit on an overseas operation, there will be an inflow of income to the UK thus improving the income balance. If a Polish worker in the UK sends some of their earnings back to their family in Poland, this represents an outflow of income which will worsen the income balance.

4. **Secondary income balance** also known as *net transfer balance* includes central government transfers to international organisations such as the IMF, UN and EU, as well as foreign aid.

Questions

1. What is the difference between the budget balance and the current account balance?

2. For each of the following scenarios, identify which section of the current account is affected, and whether an inflow or outflow occurs. Also comment on whether the current account improves or worsens as a result.

   (a) Cars from the Nissan factory in Sunderland are sold to a French car retailer for sale in France.

   (b) The UK government increases its development aid spending.

   (c) Barclays receives repayments (with the agreed rate of interest) from a Swedish company.

   (d) A British manufacturer hires a Dutch company to audit their company accounts.

● Application: **The state of the current account**

Achieving a surplus on the current account balance was a major macroeconomic policy objective of the UK government for much of the post-war era. Governments believed that in order to buy goods and services from the rest of the world you must export at least as many goods and services or you would be unable to obtain the necessary foreign currency to import without selling off foreign assets, or accumulate excessive

Table 5.1: Summary of the UK current account balance in 2014

	£bn
Exports of goods	295.4
Imports of goods	419.1
Exports of services	219.8
Imports of services	130.6
Balance of trade in goods and services	-34.6
Primary income balance	-33.1
Secondary income balance	-25.2
Current Account Balance	**-92.9**

Source: ONS, *UK Pink Book 2015*

Figure 5.1 UK current account balance as percentage of nominal GDP, 1995 to 2015

Source: ONS, *UK Pink Book 2016*

Figure 5.2: UK trade in goods and services balance, current prices, 1995 to 2015, percentage of nominal GDP

Source: ONS, *UK Pink Book 2016*

Figure 5.3: Top 10 UK export destinations

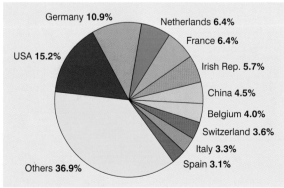

Source: ONS, year to November 2016

levels of debt. From the mid-1980s, however, a combination of the City of London drawing in vast amounts of foreign capital, the evolution of a more complex financial system and more relaxed attitude to debt meant that the current account balance became less important as a macroeconomic policy objective. The UK has had a current account deficit every year since 1984. Since the financial crisis of 2008, however, the view that a persistent current account deficit is unsustainable in the long run has become popular once again. Table 5.1 shows that the UK economy has a significant current account deficit, caused primarily by a large trade in goods deficit.

Trade is of vital importance to the UK economy. The UK has a long history of supporting free trade and remains one of the most open advanced economies. The value of exports and imports were slightly above 30% of GDP in 2016. The UK is the world's second largest exporter of services and has run a balance of trade in services surplus since 1966. However, the UK has experienced a prolonged decline in competitiveness for exporting goods, leading to a record trade in goods deficit in 2014 of £123.7bn.

Figure 5.2 shows that over the last 20 years the trade in services surplus has grown while the trade in goods deficit has worsened. For the period shown the trade in goods deficit has worsened more quickly than the trade in services surplus has improved, causing the overall trade balance to have a persistent deficit.

Despite globalisation, the majority of the UK's trade is done with her neighbours. The EU accounted for just under half of the UK's goods exports in 2015. The amount of trade between the UK and the EU has risen considerably since the UK joined in 1973, but the US, the world's largest economy, remains the largest buyer of UK exports. Most EU countries have experienced sluggish growth in recent years, particularly since the financial crisis of 2008, and the subsequent Eurozone debt crisis. This dashed hopes that the

Figure 5.4: Top 10 UK import sources

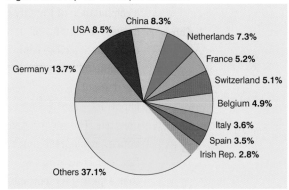

Source: ONS, year to November 2016

Figure 5.5 UK goods exports to the EU and non-EU areas, percentage of total UK goods exports, current prices, 1999 to 2015

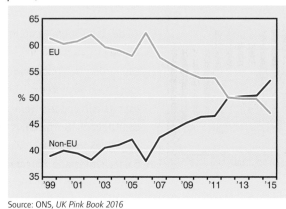

Source: ONS, *UK Pink Book 2016*

Figure 5.6: UK trade in goods and services balance with the EU and selected EU countries, 1999 to 2015

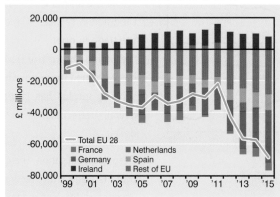

Source: ONS

Imports to the UK from emerging economies have risen considerably in recent years, with China now being the second largest source of imports.

depreciation of Sterling in 2007 could bring an export-led recovery. Furthermore, most economists agree that the UK needs to re-orient exports towards faster growing emerging markets, as Germany has done. Imports to the UK from emerging economies have risen considerably in recent years, with China now being the third largest source of imports as shown in Figure 5.4. Therefore, most economists agree that the UK needs to rebalance its trade with these economies by exporting more to them. UK goods exports to non-EU countries have grown at a faster rate than UK goods exports to the EU. Between 2007 and 2015, goods exports to non-EU countries rose by 54% while goods exports to EU countries rose by only 15%.

In addition, the UK has a substantial trade deficit with the EU, as shown in Figure 5.6, but a trade surplus with several non-EU countries, shown in Figure 5.7.

Those in favour of Brexit would argue that trading less with the EU, and trading more with the rest of the World, would create the potential for significant export growth, while our trade deficit with EU countries would be cut, leading to an overall improvement in the trade balance. Whether this will happen or not, depends of the trade deals the UK manages to negotiate.

Figure 5.7: UK trade in goods and services balance with selected non-EU countries, 1999 to 2015

Source: ONS, *UK Pink Book 2015*

Figure 5.8: Trade in goods

Source: ONS, *UK Pink Book 2015*

Figure 5.9: Trade in oil balance

Source: ONS, *UK Pink Book 2015*

Figure 5.10: UK balance of trade in services

Source: ONS, *UK Pink Book 2015*

(a) The balance of trade in goods

The UK trades similar items with the rest of the world. The most important traded items for the UK are mechanical machinery, oil (crude and refined), electrical machinery and pharmaceuticals. The UK has traditionally run a trade in goods deficit, and the last 10 years has been no exception, as shown in Figure 5.8. Although the value of exports has grown, reaching a record high in 2012, the value of imports has risen by more, hence the record goods deficit in that year.

Since the discovery of North Sea oil in the 1980s, net exports of this commodity, as well as natural gas, prevented trade in goods from going further into deficit. Since 2005 however, the UK has run a deficit on its trade in oil balance, as shown in Figure 5.9. The deficit on trade in oil is set to grow as stocks decline over the next decade, with an estimated fall in output of 6% per annum.

(b) UK balance of trade in services

The UK has run a trade in services surplus every year since 1966. This is mainly because the UK has a **comparative advantage** in services, with financial services playing an especially important role, accounting for around 22.5% of UK service exports in 2015. The English language also makes exports of other professional services such as consultancy and advertising competitive. The level of total UK trade in goods as a proportion of total trade in goods and services has been gradually declining since peaking at 75% in 1985. This is consistent with the rising share of UK trade in services, 44% of total trade in 2015, indicative of the UK's relative strength in services activities.

However, services are not as tradable as goods, and there are greater legal and language barriers for trading services internationally. As a result the value of trade in services is less than that for goods, and the trade in services surplus does not offset the trade in goods deficit, resulting in an overall trade deficit, as was shown in Figure 5.2.

A major cause for concern is the UK's high degree of **import penetration**. Import

Figure 5.11: UK import penetration

Source: OECD

The English language makes exports of professional services such as consultancy and advertising competitive.

volumes into the UK as a percentage of final expenditure have been on a generally upward trend over the last 15 years (as shown in Figure 5.11). UK demand for imports is **income elastic**, so a change in income will result in a more than proportional change in the value of imports purchased. This explains the fall in import penetration in 2009, as recession took full effect. Despite weak or even negative real household income growth since 2010 (see Chapter 4), UK import penetration remains significantly higher than the vast majority of the UK's main trading partners. Combined with the relative decline of manufacturing exports it is clear that the UK lacks competitiveness in goods. The UK's **productivity gap** (see Chapter 6) partially explains this.

Question

3. Examine two reasons for the UK's relative lack of competitiveness in goods.

(c) The primary income balance

The primary income balance was in surplus every year between 2001 and 2011 as shown by Figure 5.12. The growing credits and debits from 2002 to 2007 reflect a strong global economy, causing earnings from investments both in the UK and overseas to grow considerably. The 2008 financial crisis and the subsequent period of slower global growth caused a fall in earnings from investments inside and outside the UK. The main cause of the UK's historical surplus on the primary income balance has been credits on direct investment income exceeding debits every year since 1986, reflecting the strong performance of UK companies operating overseas, particularly financial institutions. However, since 2012 the primary income balance turned to a growing deficit, and Figures 5.1 and 5.2 showed that the deterioration in the current account balance has become less attributable to the trade balance and more attributable to the decline in the primary income balance. This suggests that UK earnings on assets overseas fell in value relative to the earnings of foreign investors in the UK. The recent deterioration in the primary income balance can be attributed to the decline

Figure 5.12: UK primary income balance

Source: ONS, *UK Pink Book 2016*

in the direct investment income balance, meaning that inflows of income to the UK from profits, interest and dividends, relative to outflows, have declined substantially. This is partly due to the UK's relatively strong performance between 2013 and 2015 relative to other EU countries causing holdings of UK assets to yield a relatively higher return. Some economists point to foreign takeovers and ownership of companies operating in the UK as a reason for a deteriorating primary income balance, as profits from their UK operations flow overseas.

Figure 5.13: Secondary income balance

Source: ONS, *UK Pink Book 2016*

(d) Secondary income balance

The final and smallest component of the current account is the secondary income balance, formerly known as the net transfer balance. As an advanced economy the UK is a net donor of international aid, and a net contributor to the budgets of international institutions such as the UN, World Bank and most significantly, the EU. As a result, the UK runs a deficit in the net secondary income balance, which has grown larger in recent years.

● Analysis: **The current account balance during the last decade**

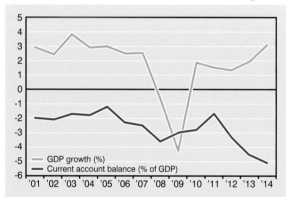

Figure 5.14: UK current account balance and GDP growth

Source: HM Treasury and ONS

Figure 5.14 shows changes in the current account balance over time. It is clear to see that changes in the current account balance are **counter-cyclical**. That is, when growth rises, the current account balance tends to worsen, and the opposite is true when growth falls. During an upswing or a boom, consumers usually see a rise in their real incomes, and thus they will spend more and some of this increase will be spent on imports. UK consumers have a high marginal propensity to import, and thus this effect will be significant. Furthermore, when the domestic economy is booming firms face capacity constraints, and will tend to focus on the domestic market, thus reducing exports. During a recession, domestic firms tend to focus more on exporting to overseas markets, as domestic sales struggle due to falling real incomes.

Looking more closely within the time period, and accounting for factors other than UK GDP growth, we can identify some clear patterns emerging.

(i) 2008-2011: This period was one of recession (2008-09) followed by an anaemic recovery. Although the trade balance improved from 2008 to 2009 as consumers and businesses reduced their spending on imports during the recession and the collapse in the value of the pound, the current account balance remained in deficit, and the trade in goods deficit reached £109bn in 2012, showing just how dependent the UK economy has become on imported goods. The fact that the UK's main trading partners were also in recession or struggling to grow during this period meant that export growth was very weak.

(ii) 2012-2016: Despite the trade in services surplus growing to a record £89.1bn in 2014, these years saw large and growing current account deficits at record levels. The trade in goods deficit worsened to £123.7bn in 2014 but the overall trade deficit, as a percentage of GDP has actually fallen from 2008 to 2015. The main reason for the worsening of the current account deficit to a worrying 5.4% of GDP in 2015 was the significant worsening of the primary income balance, as outflows of investment income were significantly higher than inflows.

In summary, despite growth in the trade in services over the past decade, the current account balance has been in permanent deficit, due to the large trade in goods deficit which has grown considerably. Furthermore despite going through the deepest recession since the 1930s, and the biggest squeeze in household incomes since at least the early 1960s, the UK has continued to run a large current account deficit throughout. This suggests that the UK has a **structural current account deficit** due to a *lack of competitiveness in goods manufacturing*.

The main reasons for the UK current account deficit are:

● The UK has a high marginal propensity to import. The UK is a consumer-driven economy, and consumers have a taste for imported goods and services.

● A strong pound during the NICE decade (1997-2007), coupled with a growing comparative disadvantage in heavy manufacturing, made UK manufacturing uncompetitive and large parts of the manufacturing sector disappeared in the UK. Once the manufacturing base has been lost, it is difficult to re-establish, a point made by James Dyson.

● Growth of the UK's main export partners in the Eurozone had been weak even before the financial crisis of 2008 and subsequent Eurozone debt crisis. This has hindered export growth considerably.

● The UK has experienced high import penetration due to globalisation and the industrialisation of developing economies such as China and India.

● Poor non-price competitiveness due to inferior quality or reliability of UK goods, partly due to weak product innovation.

● The UK's comparative advantage has shifted to services, and while the UK has a large and growing trade in services surplus, exporting services is more difficult, leading to an overall trade deficit.

There are many theories as to why UK firms are less competitive than their rivals in Germany or Japan, the world's second and third largest net exporters (after China). Research shows that UK firms have, on average, lower productivity and lower levels of investment. This is at least partly due to 'excessive' executive pay. Boardroom remuneration packages are second only to top managers in the US, and up to five times that of top Japanese or German managers. Arguably this 'crowds-out' funds for investment. More importantly, UK companies tend towards the publicly-owned model. Many argue that publically-owned companies adopt a more 'short termist' approach, favouring cost cutting and short term profit to be distributed as dividends. German and Japanese companies on the other hand tend more towards a privately-owned model, such as the German *Mittlestand* (small to medium sized usually family-run manufacturing companies), where managers and workers work together more closely to look after the long term interest of the company, and usually invest more in training and capital equipment. Many argue that this approach improves competitiveness in the long run.

● Evaluation: Does the current account deficit matter?

A current account deficit is traditionally thought to be undesirable. An individual cannot spend more than they earn without running down savings or borrowing. In the same way, an economy cannot buy more from the rest of the world than it sells without borrowing from overseas or reducing savings and investments abroad. In every year since 1998, the UK has borrowed from abroad to finance its continuing current account deficit. This has resulted in inward investment (UK liabilities) exceeding outward investment (UK assets). However, the City of London has attracted so much direct and portfolio investment over the last 30 years that the UK has received enough financial capital to pay for her current account deficit. That said, the financial sector tends to be volatile, and financial companies are highly mobile, especially with strong competition from Shanghai, Dubai and New York, who compete with London as the base for global finance. Many point to the resilience of the City of London, not least due to its desirable time zone location between New York and East Asia, the use of the English language and a reliable legal system, but relying on the financial sector to enable the UK to pay for its current account deficit may not be a sustainable approach. After the vote to leave the EU on the 23rd June 2016, there is a possibility that UK-based banks could lose the automatic right to trade in EU states, known as 'passporting', along with the right to process transactions in euros, if the UK leaves the single market. This puts at risk not just the inward FDI flows needed to sustain a current account deficit, but the very survival of the City of London as one of the World's leading financial centres.

It is also important to examine how large the current account deficit is as a percentage of total national income, or GDP. If the current account deficit is less than 5% of GDP, it is generally thought to be manageable, especially for a relaitvely creditworthy economy such as the UK. Indeed, many would argue that a current account deficit shows that UK consumers are enjoying a large amount of overseas goods and services, which improve living standards. If the deficit exceeds 5% of GDP, as it did in 2014 and 2015, then there is a greater cause for concern. The UK's current account deficit is on the edge of what most economists consider to be 'manageable limits'.

Although it is hoped the economy will not run a deficit indefinitely, the large and persistent trade in goods deficit

London has strong competition from Shanghai, Tokyo and New York as the base for global finance.

does indicate a *structural weakness in the UK economy, particularly in manufacturing*. Since the 2008 financial crisis the major political parties and the Bank of England have repeatedly called for a *re-balancing of the economy; away from consumption and imports, towards investment and exports*. It was hoped that the fall in consumer spending and rising savings ratio after the financial crisis coupled with a fall in the value of the pound would start this process, but the record trade in goods deficit in 2015 shows that if the re-balancing process does occur, it will take some time. The waning demand for UK exports from struggling Eurozone economies has not helped, but more fundamental changes which increase investment and reduce the *productivity gap* are also needed (see Chapter 6 on this latter topic).

Questions

4. Explain the causes of the UK trade deficit.

5. Evaluate the view that the UK's current account deficit is a major cause for concern.

● Analysis: **The changing value of the pound**

The value of the pound relative to the value of the currencies of the UK's main trading partners is shown in Figure 5.15. The Sterling Exchange Rate Index (ERI) assigns each currency a weighting according to the proportion of trade the UK does with each country. As a result, changes in the ERI show what has happened to the value of Sterling on a trade-weighted index. The pound operates in a **floating exchange rate**

Figure 5.15: Indices for Sterling ERI, Euro/£ and Dollar/£ rates (02 Jan 2007 = 100)

Source: Bank of England

system, meaning the Bank of England does not deliberately intervene in setting the value of the pound. The exchange rate is determined by the supply and demand for the pound. The exchange rate appreciated between 1996 and 2001, and then remained broadly constant until 2006, when the value of the pound rose again. The exchange rate fell dramatically, by almost 30% between late 2007 and early 2009. Since then, the pound gradually appreciated against other major currencies before depreciating markedly after the Brexit vote on 23rd June 2016, as shown in Figure 5.16.

Figure 5.16: Sterling exchange rates

Source: Bank of England, November 2016 inflation report

The reasons for these changes are outlined below:

1996-late 2007: During this period the pound was generally strengthening or remaining at a high level. This was due to:

- Confidence in UK economic growth and macroeconomic policy framework leading to speculative buying of pounds.

- During this period the Bank of England had higher interest rates than the ECB, Bank of Japan, and at times, the Federal reserve. This led to an inflow of **hot money**.

- The City of London attracted vast inflows of FDI during this period, raising demand for pounds.

- The US trade deficit weakened the dollar, which boosted Sterling's trade-weighted exchange rate.

Late 2007-mid 2009: The value of the pound plummeted during this period due to:

- The UK entered a deep recession which reduced confidence in the UK economy, causing speculators to sell pounds.

- The 2008 financial crisis hit the City of London especially hard, halting FDI and portfolio investment flows into the UK.

- Between July 2007 and March 2009 the base rate of interest set by the Bank of England was cut from 5.75% to 0.5%. This encouraged hot money outflows.

- A return to a more realistic value against the euro and the dollar was likely to happen sooner or later, and this adjustment occurred as a result of the financial crisis.

Mid 2009-2015: The value of the pound slowly appreciated due to:

- From a low of £1 = $1.38 in March 2009, the value of Sterling risen against the euro which is given high importance on the trade-weighted index as over 40% of the UK's trade is with the Eurozone. This has been due to the Eurozone debt crisis lowering confidence in Eurozone economies. Fears of a currency area break up caused financial capital to move from the Eurozone to the UK, which is seen as a relatively safe haven. As the recovery finally took hold from Q1 2013 through to 2015, with annualised quarterly growth rates between 2% and 4%, confidence in the UK economy grew, attracting speculation to buy pounds.

Mid 2015 – end of 2016: the value of the pound fell by 20% on the trade-weighted index due to:

- Uncertainty about the outcome of the EU referendum led speculators to sell pounds and companies to delay inward investment plans.

- The outcome of the referendum has caused a huge amount of uncertainty over the UK's future trading arrangements and economic policies leading to further speculative outflows and for the first time in a long time, net FDI outflows.

● Analysis: **What are the consequences of a weaker pound?**

- An improvement in export competitiveness.

- A potential decrease in import penetration as the price of imports rises, making domestically produced goods and services relatively cheaper.

- A rise in inflation as the cost of essential imports such as food, energy and clothing increase. Also, imported raw material costs rise for domestic firms. In the wake of the depreciation following the Brexit vote, the Bank of England forecast inflation to reach 4% in 2018, it's highest ever forecast level.

- Potentially, an export-led recovery as foreigners take advantage of cheaper goods and services produced in the UK, and UK consumers reduce the amount they purchase from overseas.

- Potentially higher profits for UK companies operating overseas, as their overseas earnings are more valuable in pound terms. This could improve the primary income balance as the profits of large UK companies grow. This could lead to higher wages, and provide funds for investment. The FTSE 100 index improved markedly during 2016 as large UK companies registered large increases in overseas earnings.

Evaluation: Does depreciation always result in an improved trade balance?

Economists are divided on whether the latest depreciation of the pound, following the Brexit vote, will lead to any substantial improvement in the trade balance. Figure 5.17 shows that following the 2008 depreciation of the pound, there was little, if any, discernable improvement in the trade balance.

Reasons why a fall in the value of Sterling may not lead to an improved trade balance include:

Figure 5.17: UK net trade in goods and services

Source: ONS

- The UK specialises in high value-added goods and services. Demand for both are relatively insensitive to price changes. The Office for Budget Responsibility estimates a 10 percent fall in the relative price of exported services will increase demand by just 2.2 per cent.

- Many UK companies are firmly built into EU and global supply chains, importing many of their raw materials and components from them. Although a weaker pound should lead UK companies to seek cheaper domestic suppliers, in practice this is not always easy.

- UK exporters often 'price to market', leaving the foreign currency price of their goods unchanged. While they would receive a bonus in sterling terms, there is not necessarily growth in the volume of exports.

- Price is just one factor that affects imports and exports. In the long term the UK needs to raise investment, product innovation and productivity. Given the uncertainty surrounding the UK's future trading arrangements following the Brexit vote, many companies are withholding investment plans, meaning the underlying causes of the UK's trade deficit are not set to improve.

Demand for imported services, however, such as foreign holidays, are highly price sensitive. At the end of 2016, The Bank of England forecast exports to grow by 2 per cent in 2017 and 1 per cent in 2018, while imports would increase by 0.25 per cent in 2017 and then fall by 1 per cent in 2018, so some improvement in the trade balance due to depreciation is likely.

Question

6. To what extent will a fall in the value of the pound improve UK macroeconomic performance?

Chapter 6

The Supply Side: Productivity and Competitiveness

This chapter examines how the UK economy has performed in terms of productivity growth and why this is an important issue. Measures to raise productivity are considered in the context of diminished competitiveness of UK firms relative to some other developed countries.

● ● Knowledge and Application: What is productivity?

Figure 6.1: UK productivity growth

Source: HM Treasury

Productivity measures the ratio of output to input, in other words the production of goods and services as a proportion of the factors of production used to make them. Although productivity can be measured for all factors of production, it is **labour productivity** which is of most concern to macroeconomists. **Labour productivity** is the ratio of output to labour input, typically measured as the total value of output (GDP) per hour worked. Using 'hours worked' rather than the employment level adjusts the data for part-time work and overtime.

Figure 6.1 shows that for much of the period 1997-2007 the UK experienced productivity growth averaging the long-run trend rate of economic growth of 2.5%. However, productivity growth fell during the recession of 2008-09 and again in 2012 and 2013, before recovering in 2014 and 2015.

● Analysis: What drives increases in productivity?

Productivity growth is a key measure of macroeconomic performance. It refers to the increase over time in the productive capacity of the macroeconomy and, therefore, drives long-run, or trend growth. We can identify a number of the determinants of labour productivity:

1. Investment in human capital

Highly-skilled and trained workers are more productive as they can produce more output in a given period of time, with less waste. Better management can also motivate workers to be more productive, and organise resources better so workers can focus on core performance. Education and training are fundamentally important in creating workers with relevant and transferable skills, and good healthcare can also boost labour productivity by keeping workers healthy and reducing the number of working days lost to illness.

2. Investment in physical capital

Fixed capital investment – spending by firms on ICT and up-to-date technologies and machinery – boosts labour productivity in two ways. Firstly, it allows some replacement of labour by capital in tasks where a machine or robot is more efficient and accurate, for example in some manufacturing tasks such as car production. Secondly, better equipment can increase the productivity of remaining workers by allowing them to better organise their time or to perform manufacturing tasks.

3. Financial capital

If investment drives productivity gains, it is crucial that firms of all sizes have access to affordable credit. This allows them to invest in the latest technologies and match competition in both domestic and international markets. The credit crisis in 2007 and its lasting impact on capital markets can be seen as one cause of the UK's 'productivity gap' (see later in the chapter).

4. Product market competition

The more firms there are competing in a market, the more likely they are forced to compete on both prices and costs. Labour costs contribute a significant proportion to total costs in most modern organisations, and therefore firms will work hard to keep unit labour costs as low as possible. The key here is labour productivity: highly-skilled workers are valuable even if their wages are higher than other workers, as their higher cost is offset (and probably outweighed) by their increased output levels.

5. Labour market competition

The negotiating power of workers is an important determinant of labour productivity. Where workers enjoy considerable bargaining power (for example when unemployment is low, or when a worker has skills in shortage in the labour market) they can push up their wages. This will increase their employer's labour costs. Similarly, in an economy where trade unions are strong there may be lower productivity levels, and policies such as minimum wage legislation can increase labour costs in the lowest-paid jobs.

6. Infrastructure

Infrastructure refers to the transport and distribution networks in an economy. Good infrastructure eases the flow of workers, raw materials and finished goods across the economy, reducing the labour hours lost to unpredictable commuting travel times, delays and fuel and driver costs incurred as output is delivered to markets. Both internal and external transport links are crucial in keeping distribution costs to a minimum, and in making the UK an attractive place to do business and attract foreign direct investment.

7. Government policies

Many of the factors already raised can be influenced by government intervention (or lack of intervention) in the markets for raw materials, financial capital, labour and transport. Research and development (R&D) spending can also be targeted through the use of tax breaks and subsidies.

● Analysis: Why is productivity growth important?

Productivity growth is important for a number of reasons:

1. Productivity growth improves living standards by increasing the level of output relative to the size of the population. This helps to explain why real incomes and real output tend to increase over time, and why each generation enjoys a wider and more affordable range of goods and services than the generation before. Productivity gains boost output per worker, and also reflect the adoption of new innovations and inventions which increase quality of life as well as standard of living.

2. Increases in productivity increase output through supply-side improvements, rather than higher aggregate demand. As long-run aggregate supply rises, output and employment levels rise without pushing up prices; indeed, the price of some goods and services may fall as their unit costs fall. Non-inflationary growth does not carry the same trade-off between output and inflationary pressures, and thus is seen as highly beneficial for (nearly) all economic agents.

3. Labour productivity is a key factor in determining international competitiveness: the ability of an economy such as the UK to produce the goods and services demanded by global consumers, firms and governments. **Unit labour costs** are a key performance measure, and are calculated by dividing average wages by average output. If the UK is able to compete strongly in international markets it will experience demand for its exports. This will avoid problems with current account imbalance and create jobs for UK-based workers and profits for UK-based firms, rather than those in other countries.

4. Finally, productivity growth can be a sign of other strengths. If labour costs are low relative to output, this can reflect an economy with well-trained, organised and motivated workers. High levels of

investment create both demand and future supply, and the incomes and profits created by economic activity will boost government's tax receipts. A strong infrastructure improves quality of life as well as keeping firms' costs low.

There are possible drawbacks to strong labour productivity growth, the main one being **structural unemployment**. This exists when the unemployed (those *seeking work*) do not have the relevant skills for the vacancies available (the firms *seeking workers*). Structural unemployment is often linked closely to shifts in technology and patterns of global production, and is most likely where workers have specific and non-transferable skills related to industries which move overseas to take advantage of cheaper labour and land (see Chapter 7).

Question

1. Paul Krugman has said that "productivity isn't everything, but in the long run it is almost everything."[1] Why is it arguable that productivity growth is the key determinant of a country's standard of living over time?

● Application: **UK versus global productivity performance**

Figure 6.2: Average productivity growth for selected G7 members. GDP per hour worked, UK = 100

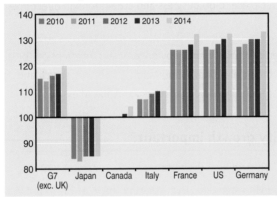

Source: ONS

Figure 6.3: Highest annual increase in productivity, 1997-2007

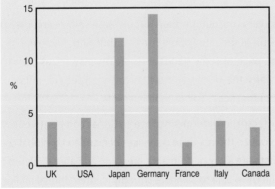

Source: HM Treasury

Figure 6.2 shows how average UK productivity growth compared with other major economies over two time periods. For the period 1997-2007 the UK experienced a growing gap in productivity against the USA, Japan and Germany. A similar trend is shown for 1997-2011, where a dramatic fall in productivity in 2009 (-14.8%) dragged down the Japan average. Note in Figure 6.2 since 2010 productivity in the UK compares unfavourably with the performance in France, the US and especially of Germany

As seen in Figure 6.4, the UK and USA have invested a lower proportion of GDP than Germany and Japan in recent years, and their productivity growth has been lower as a result. However, other economies such as France and Italy have also suffered low productivity growth despite proportionately higher levels of investment.

1. P. Krugman, *The Age of Diminished Expectations*, 1999.

Figure 6.4: Investment as % of GDP (2001-11 average) for G7 economies

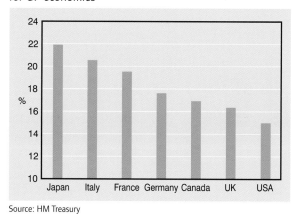

Source: HM Treasury

Question

2. Figure 6.4 shows that Italy and Japan both devoted over 20% of their GDP to investment but in Figure 6.3 the two countries differed in their experience in productivity growth. How could one explain this difference?

● Analysis: The UK productivity gap

The term '**productivity gap**' has been used in recent years to describe the loss of competitiveness of UK firms against those in similar economies. It is a key factor in the debate surrounding deindustrialisation (see Chapter 3, and Figure 3.3 in particular) and is often given as a cause of the relatively low rate of trend economic growth experienced in the UK.

A study by the London School of Economics' Centre for Economic Performance[2] identified the following key aspects of the UK productivity gap:

● Output per hour worked was almost 40% lower than in the USA and 20% lower than in Germany and France.

● Output per worker was similar in the UK and Germany, but UK labour works 16% higher hours than in Germany.

● The key factors explaining the productivity gap between the UK and France and Germany are lower capital invested per worker and lower skills.

● The productivity gap between the UK and USA is most acute in three sectors: wholesale and retailing, hotels and restaurants, and financial services.

● The productivity gap between the UK and USA was caused less by a lack of investment in labour and capital, and more by differences in managerial methods and technology.

Since 2004, the productivity gap has remained.

Table 6.1: Changes in UK productivity, 2003-12

Output per worker	7.3%
Output per job	7.4%
Output per hour	9.4%
Unit labour costs	22.9%

Source: ONS

Table 6.1 shows how although UK output has increased since 2003, in particular in terms of output per hour, unit labour costs have risen by almost a quarter over the period. Between 2006 and 2010 the UK-USA productivity gap increased by 9%, with US productivity per hour 23% higher than in the UK. Similar gaps of 18% and 16% were recorded between the UK and Germany and France respectively. Figure 6.5 compares growth in unit labour costs with other G7 economies and the eurozone average.

---

2. http://www2.lse.ac.uk/newsAndMedia/news/archives/2004/UKs_ProductivityGap.aspx

Figure 6.5: Average growth in unit labour costs, 1993-2011 and 2001-11

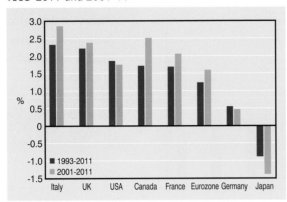

Source: HM Treasury

Figure 6.6: Sterling effective exchange rate index (January 2005 = 100)

Source: Bank of England

Figure 6.7: Producer price inflation (% change p.a.)

ONS (2016 data for September)

The UK and Italy clearly saw unit labour costs in their manufacturing sectors increase by more than the G7 and eurozone averages. In comparison, Japan saw its labour costs fall over both periods, and Germany enjoyed wage inflation of less than 1% compared to output levels.

It should be noted that this data reflects the strength of domestic currencies, or in the case of Germany, Italy and France, the strength of the euro. A stronger, or appreciating currency increases the prices of domestically-produced goods and services in overseas markets; a depreciating currency reduces the prices of domestic outputs overseas.

The relatively strong pound during 'the NICE decade' therefore could go some way in explaining comparatively poor unit labour costs, but would not explain the 'real' gap in output per hour and output per worker. Figure 6.6 shows the sterling effective exchange rate index between 2007 and 2016. This is a trade-weighted average, and therefore reflects the relative importance of different currencies. Throughout 2003 to 2008, the index had remained high, but the fall in sterling throughout 2008 should have increased UK productivity relative to other major trading partners.

The fall in the external value of sterling throughout 2016 should increase the competitiveness of UK exporters, but this could be offset by imported inflation. CPI inflation was recorded at 1.0% in September 2016, up from -0.1% the previous September and at its highest level since November 2014. Figure 6.7 shows the Producer Price Index has risen sharply in 2016.

Analysis: The 'productivity puzzle'

The trends in employment, unemployment and productivity levels in the UK in recent months has given rise to the term 'productivity puzzle.' With output contracting (falling real GDP in the double dip recession), economists would expect to see unemployment rising and employment falling. However, in the final months of 2012 the UK saw rising employment and falling unemployment. The impact of this on UK productivity is clear: more workers producing fewer goods and services implies a fall in output per worker. This is explored further in Chapter 7, where the main causes suggested are 'labour hoarding', a collapse in investment, and falling real wages.

As discussed earlier in the chapter, UK productivity has declined in recent years despite rising real GDP and record levels of employment. This supports a view of the UK economy that much of the job creation has been in low skill work and demand is supported by imports and a wealth effect from rising property prices, predominantly in the more prosperous regions of the UK.

Questions

3. Why would you expect labour hoarding by employers to have an adverse effect on productivity?

4. If interest rates are very low why nonetheless might employers be reluctant to install new capital equipment?

Analysis and Evaluation: Minding the gap – policies to boost productivity

The causes of productivity growth were explored earlier in this chapter, and possible policies to increase productivity performance will therefore be closely linked to these.

1. Investing in human capital

Recent governments have stressed, in different ways, the importance of creating an efficient, competitive workforce with the skills and abilities necessary for the UK to compete in increasingly globalised product markets. A key debate is to what extent skills can and should be developed through private firms and free markets, or by government. The relative importance of vocational and academic skills is also open to argument. Immigration is one way of bringing higher skilled workers into the UK labour market, but this can also lead to higher unemployment even if employment is rising.

2. Investing in physical capital – the importance of financial capital

Trends in investment spending are covered in greater detail in Chapter 3, but a key determinant is the cost and availability of finance. Again, the debate hinges on whether greater government intervention will increase or decrease the cost of loans to firms. Banks were criticised during the credit crisis for easy lending during the NICE decade, and are now criticised for tightening the terms of their lending as the economy struggles to recover from recession.

In addition, the reward for research, development and investment is important: high rates of corporation tax can limit the incentive for firms to expand and adopt new technologies, as well as reducing post-tax profits which are used by some firms as a source of finance.

Free market economists argue that bureaucracy also increases unit costs and limits innovation by raising the cost of doing business in the UK. They would also argue that, in terms of research, governments have a habit of 'backing losers' and subsidies to potential innovators create a culture of state dependency with low incentives for success.

3. Increasing product market competition

This is seen by many economists as the key driver of innovation, investment and rising productivity. Globalisation and free trade expose UK firms to powerful market trends, forcing them to control their costs to compete. However, this has also led to the loss of jobs to overseas producers and production plants, with structural unemployment resulting in the UK.

4. Increasing labour market competition

The 'labour hoarding' argument given for the productivity puzzle suggests that UK labour markets may not be as flexible as expected. If firms are holding on to workers despite falling demand, this suggests the costs of redundancy are high and there may be a shortage of sufficiently skilled workers when the economy recovers.

Labour market imperfections such as the National Minimum Wage may also raise labour costs and reduce productivity, but such initiatives play an important role in creating social welfare and reducing poverty and inequality.

The UK road, rail and airport network is seriously congested, particularly around major population areas such as London and the north-west conurbation of Manchester and Liverpool.

5. Investing in infrastructure

Large scale investment projects such as new runways (or even airports) and spending on public transport can boost both short-run growth (through Keynesian-style expansion and related multiplier and accelerator effects) and long-run growth (through reducing transport costs and increasing production and distribution potential).

The UK road, rail and airport network is seriously congested, particularly around major population areas such as London and the north-west conurbation of Manchester and Liverpool.

Public spending has been limited by the 'austerity measures' which aimed to bring down public spending as a proportion of GDP but with the change in leadership after the EU referendum result the current government may implement a more expansionary approach to public spending. In the Autumn Statement in November 2016 the Chancellor, Phillip Hammond, pledged to boost the supply-side of the economy through a range of policies, including:

- A National Productivity Investment Fund of £23 billion for spending on transport, digital communications, housing and research and development.

- This will include over £1bn to reduce traffic congestion, road safety and an expressway to connect Oxford and Cambridge.

- Spending of £390 million for future transport technology investment, including £100m for testing infrastructure for driverless cars, £150m for electric and hydrogen buses, and £80m for charging points for ultra-low emission vehicles.

- £1bn to invest in full-fibre broadband and 5G mobile networks.

● ● Knowledge and Application: UK Competition Policy

The competitiveness of British business is a key driver of innovation, productivity and the efficient functioning of the modern economy. These factors in turn drive improvements in GDP and the external trade balance.

A reduction in the number of competitors can lead to firms then failing to reduce their prices when they have the opportunity to do so, because they know that such a reduction would quickly be matched by their competitors. No communication between firms is necessary and this behaviour is known as tacit collusion, leading to prices which are 'sticky downwards'.

Although much economic analysis focuses on the price effects of ineffective competition, it is important to note that evidence of inefficient competition can also, or instead, emerge in the form of lower quality, a reduced range of goods and services, and/or poorer service. Competition analysts accordingly look at the price, quality, range, service combination (PQRS) rather than focusing on price alone. Also, inefficient competition does not necessarily lead to high profits. Firms that have little to fear from competition are often inefficient, so their higher prices are eaten into by their high cost base, often including higher wages.

Competition is such an important driver of economic performance that most countries in the world, including all countries in the European Union, have created competition authorities with strong legal powers aimed at preserving or increasing the extent of competition within their borders. From 1st April 2014 the **Competition Commission (CC)** and **Office of Fair Trading (OFT)** were combined in the UK into the **Competition and Markets Authority (CMA)**. These competition powers fall into five categories.

1. **Merger Control** aims to prevent firms gaining market power as a result of acquiring control of competitors. In the UK, the CMA reviews all significant mergers with a view to prohibiting those that are likely to result in a **substantial lessening of competition**. Smaller mergers are exempt from scrutiny – i.e. if the turnover of the firm being taken over is £70m or less *and* the combined firms will have no more than 25% market share. But mergers that create a company with a combined market share of more than 25% are very often allowed as long as the market remains competitive and/or it is relatively easy for new firms to enter the market.

2. It can be harder to counter the effects of market power if it arises otherwise than as a result of a merger. In the UK, however, the CMA has the ability to undertake **Market Investigations** of sectors in which there is evidence of inadequate competition. The CMA looks to see if it can identify an **adverse effect on competition** (AEC) arising out of identifiable features of the market. If so, the CMA has extensive powers to remedy the AEC by imposing behavioural conditions or forcing companies to sell part of their business. These very strong powers are in practice used quite rarely, but they can be valuable where a market appears to be working very badly, or where privatisation has created a company with very strong market power.

3. But most countries, including the UK, have **Economic Regulators** which act as a substitute for competition where companies have **substantial market power** (SMP), most obviously where there is a natural monopoly, for instance in **the utility industries** where companies often have **a natural monopoly** in supplying energy, water etc. via wires and pipes which are expensive to duplicate. These companies may only operate if licensed to do so by the regulator, which will impose strict limits on the extent to which the company may raise prices or reduce the quality and range of its products, or the quality of its customer service. Examples of regulatory bodies in the UK are the Office for the Gas and Electricity Markets (OFGEM), water suppliers (OFWAT), the communications sector (OFCOM), railway services (ORR), air traffic services (CAA) and the NHS (Monitor).

   The use of the above three powers – merger control, market investigations and economic regulation – does not imply the existence of any misbehaviour. The problem is the existence of market power that all companies will deploy to their own advantage if they are able to do so. In contrast the other two powers, listed below, are aimed at companies that are misbehaving, either individually or collectively. If the allegations are proved then very large fines can be imposed or, in the worst cases, executives sent to prison.

4. Companies are guilty of **abuse of dominant position** if the CMA can show (a) that they are dominant in their market, and (b) that they have taken steps to eliminate the limited competition that remains by unfair means, including:

- **Price discrimination** – offering price reductions and volume discounts to those customers who may be tempted to leave you for a competitor.

- **Tying** – such as tying one product to the sale of another, being restrictive of consumer choice and depriving competitors of outlets.

- **Refusal to supply a facility that is essential for all businesses attempting to compete** – the most obvious essential facilities are in the transport industry: docks, bus stations and airports.

- **Full line forcing** – the retailer is forced to stock the whole of a manufacturer's range of products, thus leaving little or no room for competitors' products.

- **Predation** (as in preying on a victim). This behaviour includes predatory pricing – the practice of dropping prices of a product so much that smaller competitors cannot cover their costs and fall out of business – and other predatory behaviour – e.g. running new bus services at frequent intervals so as to force a new competitor out of the market.

None of the above behaviours are objectionable, of course, if they are carried out by non-dominant companies that are aggressively competing to retain customers. In practice, therefore, competition authorities have to carry out complex economic analyses in order to prove that the beneficial consequences of the behaviour (such as price cuts) are outweighed by the negative consequences (the elimination of competition). Successful investigations are relatively rare, but here are some examples:

- The European Commission fined Microsoft €497 million for including its Windows Media Player within the Microsoft Windows platform.

- In December 2016, the CMA accused Actavis, a multinational drug company, of increasing the price charged to the NHS for its hydrocortisone tablets by 12,000%, in doing so abusing its dominant position as the only supplier of this life-saving drug.

5. Finally, it is illegal to enter into **agreements**, **which prevent, restrict or distort competition**, unless specifically permitted by the competition authorities. Franchise and similar agreements are therefore often OK, but other agreements not to compete are usually prohibited. Price fixing agreements (**cartels**) are particularly deprecated, especially when they are secret, and executives who enter into such agreements are guilty of a criminal offence and can be jailed. Cleverly, however, the CMA offers very lenient treatment to the first member of a cartel which comes forward to 'blow the whistle' on the arrangement. This has proved very effective in busting several secret cartels, and no doubt deters the creation of many more.

Decisions made by the CMA can be appealed through a process of judicial review with the **Competition Appeal Tribunal** (**CAT**).

Questions

5. How can effective competition policy help to maximise growth in productivity over time?

6. Using the website of the Competition and Markets Authority (https://www.gov.uk/cma-cases), summarise a recent case study in competition policy and explain which of the 5 competition powers explained above were used to determine the outcome.

Chapter 7

Employment and Unemployment

This chapter compares two measures of the number of people out of work in the UK before examining what factors account for changes in the numbers of unemployed. The final section considers the relationship between unemployment and the rate of inflation.

● Knowledge: **Defining unemployment**

Unemployment describes the status of people who are willing, able and available for work at current wage rates who cannot find a job. The total number of workers (including both those in work and those who are not) in an economy is called the **workforce**. Unemployment can be expressed as either a level (e.g. 3 million unemployed) or as a percentage of the workforce (e.g. 10% unemployment). Economists also distinguish between people who are **economically active** and **economically inactive**. The **economically active** are those of working age (16 and over, and below the retirement age) who are in employment or are unemployed.

The **economically inactive** are those of working age who are neither employed nor unemployed, and include:

● Students in full-time education (including school, college and university students).
● Workers who have taken early retirement.
● People too ill or infirm to work.
● People who have given up searching for work or not currently seeking work (e.g. university or school leavers waiting to take up a job offer).

A contentious issue in economics is that of **full employment**. From 1945 until the 1970s, the UK government expressed a clear policy of aiming to create as high employment as possible, thereby minimising unemployment. Later in the chapter we will discuss how different economists may define 'full employment' in different ways. Indeed, some Conservative governments since the 1970s have stressed the importance of price stability (carefully controlled inflation) compared with achieving full employment.

Another important concept is that of **underemployment**. This arises when a worker is employed but at an unsatisfactory level, such as in a job for which they are overqualified or where they are employed on a part-time basis when they desire full-time work. Underemployment can be a strong feature of a recession, particularly for new entrants to the labour market (school-leavers, recent university graduates or people returning to the workforce after a career break).

Underemployment can also result from 'labour hoarding': when a firm does not make redundancies when demand falls.

● Application: **Measuring unemployment**

Unemployment is measured in two different ways in the UK.

1. The **claimant count** (**CC**) measures unemployment as **the total number of people out of working and claiming Jobseeker's Allowance (JSA)**.

   It can be argued that the claimant count understates unemployment, as some people may be out of work but not claiming benefits for reasons such as:

   ● The individual's savings are too high to make them eligible for JSA (many welfare state benefits are means-tested to some extent).

   ● Household income may be relatively high if a partner or family member is economically active.

- Some people are ineligible for JSA, for example those who have not built up sufficient National Insurance contributions in the past, or those who are not EU citizens.

- People who have left their previous job voluntarily or been dismissed for misconduct are ineligible for JSA.

- Some people may be too embarrassed to claim benefit, or do not understand that they may do so.

It is important to note that where benefit is claimed fraudulently this will increase 'unemployment' on the claimant count measure.

2. The **Labour Force Survey** (**LFS**) measures unemployment by conducting **a sample survey of over 60,000 households (and over 100,000 people) every three months**. This is the government's official preferred measure of unemployment and compares directly to data collected from all countries according to the International Labour Organisation (ILO). The LFS measure therefore allows economists to judge UK economic performance in the labour market against other economies.

The LFS categorises an individual as unemployed if they:

- Out of work.
- Actively seeking work.
- Been looking for work in the past four weeks.
- Are able to start work within two weeks.

Application: **UK unemployment data**

Figures 7.1 and 7.2 show the unemployment story for the UK economy over the past 17 years. Figure 7.1 compares Claimant Count and Labour Force Survey levels of unemployment; Figure 7.2 compares the rates of unemployment.

Figure 7.1: Labour Force Survey and Claimant Count unemployment, UK

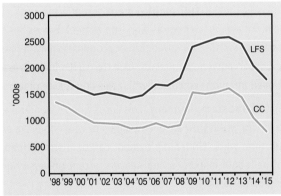

Source: HM Treasury

Figure 7.2: Labour Force Survey and Claimant Count unemployment, UK

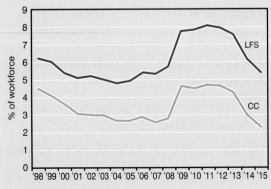

Source: HM Treasury

Analysis: **Why do the two measures of unemployment differ so much?**

The claimant count is consistently below the Labour Force Survey measure, supporting the view that the former understates unemployment. However, the differential between the measures varies, as shown in Figure 7.3, where data prior to 1998 has also been included to allow for more detailed analysis.

It is very evident that the difference between the LFS and the Claimant Count has increased over the period shown. Possible explanations for the growing divergence between the two measures are:

- Increasing benefit ineligibility (see section on Measuring unemployment above).

- The impact of long-term unemployment on job seeking; workers who remain jobless for a long period of time may become discouraged to search any longer, or reach retirement age, and therefore stop actively seeking work.

Figure 7.3: Differential between Labour Force Survey and Claimant Count measures (LFS-CC)

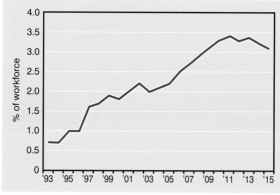

Source: HM Treasury

Figure 7.4: Claimant Count as a percentage of Labour Force Survey, UK

Source: HM Treasury

- The LFS measures members of households who may not be actively seeking work but would accept a job if available, for example parents considering a return to the workforce after taking time to raise a family.

- The stigma associated with 'benefits culture' may prevent some groups such as early retirees from claiming benefits even though they might like to find full-time work in another career or on a part-time basis to supplement income from pensions.

- Increased unemployment of higher earners (perhaps linked to increased incomes in general) which allows workers who have been made redundant to survive on savings and termination packages whilst they look for work.

Figure 7.4 shows how the CC consistently fell relative to the LFS measure between 1993 and 2008, followed by a sharp uplift during and after the recession of 2008-09. It can be argued that, during a recession, the Claimant Count increases because as major earners are made redundant, other possible earners will also become eligible for benefits.

Analysis: Causes of unemployment in the UK economy

The relationship between unemployment and economic growth is important. Both demand and supply-side factors influence the rates of job creation and job destruction across the economy. It should be noted that new employment opportunities arise even during periods of local and national decline, and there may be job losses and even the collapse of some sectors even when the economy is experiencing a boom.

The difference between those jobs created and those lost will therefore determine the net impact on unemployment in a region or across the United Kingdom.

A key issue in labour markets in rapidly evolving and changing economies is that of the mismatch between the skills of workers losing their jobs and those needed to be successful in finding work in sectors and roles where there are vacancies.

As seen on Figures 7.1, 7.2 and 7.3, UK unemployment has varied widely even over the relatively short period of the past 20 years. Those years can be divided into the following periods:

1993-2004: Stable economic growth

Unemployment fell consistently over this period, with the Labour Force Survey measure in 2004 at less than half of that recorded in 1993 as the economy began its recovery from recession.

The major downward driver of unemployment was, of course, strong and stable economic growth. The departure of sterling from the Exchange Rate Mechanism in 1992 effectively devalued the pound by around 15% against the other major European economies, allowing an export-led boom to create demand for UK goods abroad, in turn creating jobs for UK-based workers. By 1997 the UK had entered the 'NICE decade', where globalisation, high business and consumer confidence buoyed by positive wealth effects arising from housing market and stock market booms, and a powerful new faith in the abilities of the fiscal and monetary authorities created a low inflation, high growth platform for job creation.

Another important factor, this time on the supply-side of the economy, was the introduction of labour market policies aimed at creating increasing job opportunities. The New Labour government elected in 1997 quickly introduced the **New Deal** in 1998, a 'welfare to work' or 'workfare' programme designed to increase employability in groups such as unemployed youths, the long-term unemployed, lone parents and the disabled.

The New Deal introduced the ability to remove benefits from people unwilling to take up 'reasonable employment'. After 6 months, for example, all 18-24 year olds claiming Job Seeker's Allowance were expected to take up a subsidised work placement, a place in full-time education or training, or participate in either the Community Task Force or the Environmental Task Force (both designed to put spare labour to use in the local community or voluntary sector, at the same time as giving skills and experience to the young jobless).

Policies such as the National Minimum Wage (1999) and Working Families and Children's Tax Credits (1999, amended 2003) were designed to reward employment through higher pay and lower tax payments respectively. An important consideration for the unemployed is the **replacement ratio: the difference between earned and unearned income**. For lower-skilled workers, generous benefits payments may make taking up a job opportunity irrational, once taxes, travel, equipment and clothing and possibly the costs of childcare are taken into account. By increasing the replacement ratio, a greater incentive to work is created and unemployment should fall (providing there are sufficient opportunities for employment).

Figure 7.5: Change in employment levels, public and private sector

Source: ONS   *2016 Forecast

Other trends contributed to the *flexibility of the UK workforce*. Growth in part-time employment through the 1990s and beyond, typically but not exclusively for working parents, helped to reduce unemployment, as did the greater wage flexibility provided by the erosion of trade union powers throughout the 1980s. Greater education, training and retraining opportunities help workers to develop, maintain and adapt their skills to the demands of the modern workplace and reduce their susceptibility to structural changes and resulting unemployment.

Figure 7.6: Total employment by sector in the UK (public versus private)

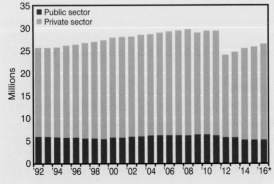

Source: ONS   *Forecast

The *growth of the public sector*, and public sector employment was a key characteristic of the New Labour years. Figure 7.5 shows the change in public sector and private sector employment between 1993 and 2016.

Between 2001 and 2005, public sector employment rose significantly faster than the private sector. However, in terms of total employment, it should be noted that the private sector remained – and remains – the major employer in the UK economy (see Figure 7.6).

Figure 7.7: UK Youth Claimant Count unemployment (000s, 18-24 year olds, 6 months+)

Source: HM Treasury

Figure 7.8: Long-term (25 years old +, >24 months unemployment) and Youth (18-24, >6 months unemployment) unemployment in the UK

Source: HM Treasury

Demographic and education sector trends also played a part in reducing unemployment. With a decline in the birth rate since the late 1960s, and increasing numbers of 16-24 years olds taking up places in further and higher education, youth unemployment declined dramatically during this period.

2005-2009: Slowdown in growth

The key contributor to employment and unemployment figures in the period 2005 to 2009 was the slowdown in economic growth experienced by the UK economy.

As the economy grew throughout the first half of the NICE decade, unemployment fell. However, as growth dropped below the trend rate in 2005 unemployment began to rise, with a predictably dramatic rise experienced in 2009 before the economy moved out of recession in 2010. The data for particular sectors of the labour market provides a more detailed picture of how recession affected certain workers as shown in Figures 7.7 and 7.8.

Both measures more than doubled between 2008 and 2010, and the impact on youth unemployment in particular has been covered widely in the press. The phenomenon of the 'NEETs': **16-24 year olds not in employment, education or training** is of great concern and could create a 'mini-generation' of young people facing atrophied skills and a lack of experience in the workplace. It is possible that, even if the economy recovers relatively quickly, this current cohort of NEETs will be passed over for new jobs as new school and university leavers enter the labour market.

Question

1. How does the data in Figures 7.7 and 7.8 illustrate the concern over the phenomenon of the NEETs?

2009 onwards

Figure 7.1 showed how UK unemployment rose throughout the recession of 2008-09, albeit with a time lag of a few months. Between mid-2008 and mid-2009, the LFS measure recorded an increase in joblessness of 1 million. Even when the economy returned to slow growth in 2010, unemployment remained high around the 2.6 million level.

Declining productivity when GDP growth declines can be explained by factors such as:

- 'Labour hoarding': businesses hold onto workers because they are expecting the economy to return to stronger growth imminently and they wish to avoid the costs associated with making redundancies and then re-hiring high quality workers. This can be a positive sign for the macroeconomy.

- Collapse in investment due to the banking crisis: if firms are finding cheap credit difficult to obtain, this

Figure 7.9: Annual change in output per worker, UK, 2005-15

Source: ONS

Figure 7.10: LFS employment (millions)

Source: ONS

will have hindered investment in capital which can boost labour productivity. This links to the third point, below:

● Falling real wages: a combination of a squeezed labour market and relatively high inflation has made hiring or retaining workers a more cost-effective solution than investing in more efficient technologies and capital.

● 'Zombie firms': this argument is that there are firms in the UK which remain in existence despite very low levels of output and invest-ment. These firms are able to meet their debt repayments only because of very low interest rates, and they are not creating surplus profit required to fund investment programmes.

● Analysis: Why does UK employment continue to rise?

The UK labour market has remained resilient despite the uneven recovery from the Great Recession as shown in Figure 7.10. Employment has continued to grow, even after the surprise result of the EU referendum in June 2016 and the subsequent depreciation in sterling. However, recent trends within the picture of overall growth in job creation should be highlighted:

● The phenomenon of zero hours contracts and the 'gig economy': as some sectors (taxi drivers, household services, some business functions) have seen growth in self-employment and freelance work, firms have been able to maintain or increase employment levels by shifting some of the non-wage costs of employing workers (pension contributions, entitlement to holiday and sick pay, or even paid breaks) from the firm to the worker

● Falling living standards: changes to benefit eligibility, greater job insecurity and low or negative real wage growth has led to growth in the 'squeezed middle' of households which, despite being in work, are not experiencing increases in their standard of living and quality of life

● The impact of 'Brexit' and wider political trends towards greater protectionism will have an impact on the UK labour market in the years ahead as possible changes in the pattern of migration within the EU, and the rest of the world, arise

● Analysis: Is there a trade-off between unemployment and inflation?

This section leads into the following chapter on inflation and deflation. Since the work of A W Phillips in the 1950s, there has been debate in economics around the exact relationship between two key macro-economic variables: unemployment and inflation. The stable, negative correlation (**the Phillips curve**) was an important belief of the Keynesian school.

Table 7.1 shows data for unemployment and inflation data for the UK economy in recent years.

Table 7.1: 'Phillips Curve' data: unemployment and inflation

	LFS Unemployment (% of workforce)	Consumer Price Inflation (% p.a.)		LFS Unemployment (% of workforce)	Consumer Price Inflation (% p.a.)
1993	10.4	2.5	2005	4.9	2.0
1994	9.5	2.0	2006	5.4	2.3
1995	8.6	2.6	2007	5.3	2.3
1996	8.1	2.5	2008	5.7	3.6
1997	6.9	1.8	2009	7.7	2.2
1998	6.2	1.6	2010	7.8	3.3
1999	6.0	1.4	2011	8.1	4.5
2000	5.4	0.8	2012	8.0	2.8
2001	5.1	1.2	2013	7.6	2.6
2002	5.2	1.3	2014	6.2	1.5
2003	5.0	1.4	2015	5.4	0.0
2004	4.8	1.4			

Source: HM Treasury

Exercise

2. Use the data from Table 7.1 to plot a Phillips curve with rate of unemployment on the horizontal axis and inflation on the vertical axis. How stable is the relationship that you have drawn between the level of unemployment and the rate of price inflation?

Economists have identified the **NAIRU** (the **n**on-**a**ccelerating **i**nflation **r**ate of **u**nemployment) as a useful point of reference. The theory suggests that any attempt to reduce unemployment below a certain level will lead to an increase in inflationary pressure. This is a similar concept to the Natural Rate of Unemployment, which suggests perhaps that there is an 'equilibrium' level of unemployment in the economy. Classical, or supply-side economists, argue that this unemployment persists not due to a lack of demand, but rather due to supply-side imperfections in the labour market such as excessive trade union power, minimum wage legislation, and an unwillingness on the part of the unemployed to actively search for work and take responsibility for their own joblessness.

Keynesian economists on the other hand stress the importance of demand-management policies such as fiscal and monetary expansion to increase aggregate demand (actual GDP) in the economy to create sufficient demand for labour and reduce unemployment.

The relationship between inflation and unemployment is actually a relationship of each variable to the central policy objective of economic growth. In times of strong GDP growth, unemployment tends to fall and inflationary pressure rises; in times of low or negative growth, unemployment rises and inflationary pressure recedes.

The data in Table 7.1 does not show a clear linear relationship because not all unemployment is caused by a lack of growth (structural and frictional factors also exist) and not all inflation is caused by excessive demand (cost-push pressures can also increase prices, as experienced in the recent recession where CPI remained stubbornly above its upper target of 3% until 2012).

Questions

3. 'Most unemployment in an economy such as the UK is cyclical.' To what extent do you agree with this statement?
4. To what extent is unemployment the key macroeconomic indicator to explain living standards in an economy?

Chapter 8

Inflation and Deflation

This chapter looks at the difference between the Retail Price Index and the Consumer Price Index, as well as how they portray trends in price changes over the last decade. The chapter goes on to look at recent price changes in various sectors before comparing UK inflation with that of other countries. An examination of the fluctuations in the rate of inflation over the last 10 years follows before a final discussion on the dangers of deflation.

● ● Knowledge and Application: Defining and measuring UK inflation

Inflation is defined as a sustained increase in the general price level.

A key point to note here is that the price of some goods and services might be falling, but the average price of goods and services in the economy are rising. As prices rise, the value of a given amount of money falls as it can purchase fewer goods and services.

There are two main measures of inflation in the UK:

1. Consumer Price Index (CPI)

The CPI index has been used to measure the official rate of inflation in the UK since December 2003 (previously it was the Retail Price Index which is the second measure discussed below). The Bank of England targets inflation at 2.0% according to the CPI measure (see Chapter 9). This measure uses the same methodology as the *Harmonised Index of Consumer Prices* (*HICP*) measure, which is used by economies across the EU. The ECB uses this measure to assess rates of inflation in the Eurozone. The government switched to the CPI measure so that UK inflation could be compared directly with economies in the EU.

The CPI is a weighted index measuring the average price increase of a basket goods and services purchased by a typical household. The Office for National Statistics' (ONS) Expenditure and Food Survey measures the price changes of 700 goods and services purchased from an average household. Each item is weighted according to the proportion of household income that is spent on it. Therefore, if twice as much income is spent by households on clothes than on video games, clothing should receive twice the weighting.

To ensure that the CPI measure accurately reflects changes in the cost of living, amendments are made annually to the items that are included in the basket so that changes in consumer habits are reflected. In 2012 tablet computers were included for the first time, while processed film was excluded. Similarly, changes are made to the weightings

Figure 8.1: CPI group weightings 1996 (parts of 1000)

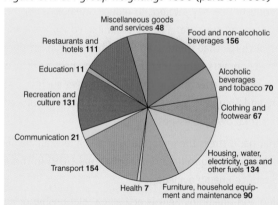

Source: ONS

Figure 8.2: CPI group weightings 2016 (parts of 1000)

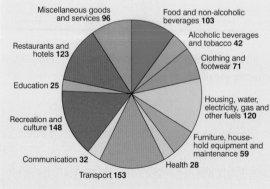

Source: ONS

that items receive each year. In 2016 for example, gas bills were given a lower weighting due to falls in gas prices over the previous year causing households to spend a smaller proportion of their income on gas.

2. Retail Price Index (RPI)

The RPI was the official measure of inflation from 1947 to 2003. The RPI is measured in a very similar way to the CPI, but also includes some items omitted in the CPI, such as council tax, mortgage interest payments and buildings insurance. As a result, many believe that the inclusion of vital housing costs makes the RPI a better measure of changes in the average cost of living of UK households. The RPI is still used by the government for various purposes such as to set rent increases in social housing, and to calculate amounts payable on index-linked gilts. Furthermore, employers often use the RPI as a basis for discussions on wage increases.

> ## Questions
>
> 1. Calculate the percentage change in the proportional of household expenditure on (i) clothing and footwear, and (ii) transport, between 1996 and 2016.
>
> 2. Explain the possible causes of a decrease in the share of household spending on food and non-alcoholic beverages between 1996 and 2016.
>
> 3. Explain the reasons why the share of household spending on transport remained broadly constant.

● Knowledge: **Explaining differences between the RPI and CPI**

There are some important distinctions in the way these two indices are measured:

1. There is an important statistical difference in how the RPI and CPI measures are calculated; the CPI uses a geometric mean, while the RPI uses an arithmetic mean.

2. The CPI excludes some vital housing costs that are included in the RPI, namely Council tax, mortgage interest payments, house depreciation, buildings insurance, ground rent, solar PV feed in tariffs and other house purchase costs such as estate agents' and conveyance fees.

3. The RPI index excludes some items included in the CPI measure, such as university tuition fees and stockbroker fees.

4. The weightings given in the CPI index are based on the spending patterns of all households in the UK, tourists visiting the UK, and those living in institutional accommodation such as university halls of residence. CPI weightings are based on household spending in the National Accounts. On the contrary, the RPI weightings are based on the Expenditure and Food Survey. Furthermore, the RPI excludes the top 4% of households in the income distribution and pensioners, as their consumption patterns are significantly different to the rest of the population. Therefore, the CPI covers a broader section of the population.

● ● Application **and** Analysis: **Explaining the difference between trends in the CPI and RPI**

Figure 8.3 shows that since the introduction of CPI inflation as the official measure in 2003, RPI has generally been higher. This is due to:

1. The inclusion of housing costs in RPI

Housing costs tend to rise more quickly than general prices, thus causing the RPI to measure a higher rate of inflation. In 2009 however, the RPI plummeted, showing a brief period of negative inflation. This was

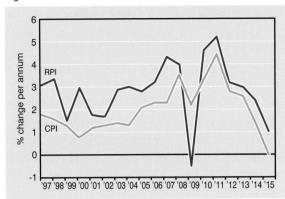

Figure 8.3: UK CPI and RPI inflation (1997-2015)

Source: HM Treasury

due to dramatic cuts in interest rates, from 5.0% in April 2008 to 0.5% in March 2009, which reduced mortgage interest payments considerably.

2. The different 'mean' calculations

An arithmetic mean ($\Sigma x/n$), used in calculating the RPI, tends to give a higher figure than a geometric mean ($((X1)(X2)\ldots (Xn))^{1/n}$), which is used in the CPI. According to the ONS, the different calculation of the 'mean' is the most important reason inflation on the RPI measure tends to be higher than that calculated by the CPI.

● Evaluation: Problems with using RPI or CPI indices

There are several problems with using the RPI or CPI as accurate measures of inflation. They are:

1. The CPI and RPI both measure the *average* rate of inflation, faced by a *typical* household. In reality, individuals and households have very different consumption baskets, and thus face different rates of inflation.

2. Both measures do not take into account changes in the quality of goods and services, and thus might overstate inflation. If you bought a car today you would get a lot more for your money compared to a car purchased in 1970 e.g. electric windows, central locking, airbags, a GPS navigation system etc.

3. After CPI was adopted as the official measure of inflation in 2003, many public and private sector employers started to use CPI inflation as a basis for wage negotiation rather than RPI, indexing wage increases to the CPI rate. When the two indices were close together in 2004-5 this was not much of a problem, but in 2006-7 when RPI outpaced CPI the policy to use CPI became controversial, as many felt they were receiving *real* pay cuts. However, when RPI fell well below CPI in 2008-09, those same employees were arguably receiving pay rises in real terms. Whether the CPI or RPI best reflect the cost of living increases faced by employees depends on a number of factors, but home ownership is undoubtedly very important. For those with mortgages the RPI is likely to be a more accurate measure, as mortgage interest payments are included. This highlights a key problem; it is very difficult to find a measure that accurately reflects cost of living changes for whole groups of employees.

● ● Application and Analysis: Recent trends in UK inflation

Inflation according to the RPI measure peaked at 9.5% in 1990 at the end of the so called 'Lawson boom'. Between 1992 and 2004 inflation was very stable according to all measures. Shortly after being given their independence in 1998 the Bank of England wanted to show that they were tough on inflation, and raised the base rate of interest from 5.9375% in April to 7.25% in November of that year, quelling fears that strong growth at that time would lead to rising inflation. This rate rise, combined with other factors (explained later) caused inflationary pressures to subside. Between 1997 and 2003 the base rate of interest was historically very stable, and fell during this period reaching 3.5% in July 2003, as seen in Figure 8.4. Between late 2003 and mid 2007 inflationary pressures grew and both CPI and RPI increased, as shown in Figure 8.3. To counter this, the Bank of England raised the base rate of interest incrementally from 3.5% in November 2003 to 5.75% in July 2007. After overshooting the 'acceptable limit' of 3% in March 2007 (3.1%), CPI inflation fell below target to 1.8% by September of that year. From then, however, inflation rose considerably, reaching 5.2% according to the CPI measure by September 2008. Inflation then collapsed,

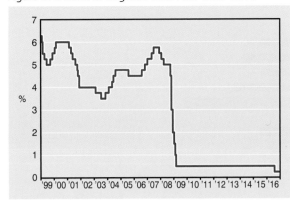

Figure 8.4: Bank of England base rate 1999-2016

Source: Bank of England

Figure 8.5: CPI in goods, services and overall 1999-2015

Source: ONS

plummeting to 1.1% (CPI) by September 2009. To prevent a sustained period of deflation, the Bank of England slashed the base rate during 2008 and early 2009, reaching just 0.5% by March of 2009, where it remained until August 2016 despite CPI inflation climbing to 5.2% by September 2011. Inflation then subsided, reaching 2.4% by June 2012 and then falling further, driven by plummeting oil and other commodity prices. CPI inflation averaged 0% for 2015, and remained well below the 2% target throughout 2016. In August 2016 the Bank of England changed the base rate for first time since March 2009, cutting the rate to just 0.25% in an attempt to reduce possible deflationary pressures that would result from a downturn, which many expected to follow the Brexit vote.

So far we have looked only at overall inflation for goods and services. However, once we disaggregate the data, we can reveal a number of trends which are hidden by aggregate inflation figures:

1. Figure 8.5 shows that for most of the period 1999 to 2016, goods inflation was considerably lower than services inflation. In fact, according to the CPI measure, the average price of goods was falling between 2000 and 2004. Services, by contrast, saw steady price increases of around 3.5-4.5% per annum throughout the period. This means that the cause of low inflation between 1997 and 2004 was due to minimal price rises of goods, while inflation in services was present throughout this period.

2. From 2005 goods inflation started an upward trajectory. Despite falls in goods inflation from 2008 to 2009, goods inflation increased quite dramatically, rising above the rate of services inflation by 2011. Therefore, it was abnormally high inflation in goods, rather than services, which caused overall the monthly rate of CPI inflation to break 5% in the autumns of 2008 and 2011. Since 2011 however, goods inflation has fallen by more than services inflation, bringing down overall inflationary pressure with it.

3. Figure 8.5 shows that in 2014 and 2015 goods price inflation plummeted, which weighed down on overall CPI inflation. This was mostly due to the dramatic fall in the price of oil and other commodities from the summer of 2014 feeding through into lower manufacturing costs. Service price inflation, too, was reduced. 'Cheap oil' (and gas) meant that the cost of providing transport, electricity and other services were reduced.

● **Application: International comparison of inflation rates**

During the 1970s and much of the 1980s the UK was known as 'the sick man of Europe', in part owing to her poor inflation record. Since the early 1990s the UK's inflation record has been much improved and between the mid 1990s to the mid 2000s the UK's inflation rate compared favourably to that of her competitors. However, from 2005 onwards, the UK inflation rate was generally higher than that of her main competitors, as shown in Figures 8.6, 8.7 and 8.8. Figure 8.7 shows that between 2006 and 2016 the UK's average inflation rate was above that of most advanced economies. This was in part because the Eurozone

Figure 8.6: Average annual percentage change in CPI, Nov 2006 to Sep 2016

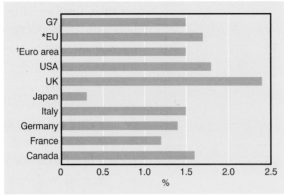

Source: OECD   *28 countries   †19 countries

Figure 8.7: Inflation rates (CPI annual % change) for selected economies 2006-2016

Source: OECD   *28 countries   †19 countries

Figure 8.8: Inflation rates (CPI annual % change) for selected countries 2006-2016

Source: OECD

economy weakened, and the threat of deflation emerged in many European economies.

Question

4. Explain why inflation rates in the UK exceeded those of her main competitors between 2006 and 2016.

● Analysis: Explanations for historically low UK inflation 1992-2017

Historically, the last 25 years has seen the UK experiencing much lower rates of inflation. In the 1970s and 1980s, double-digit inflation rates were common. There are several explanations for historically low inflation in the UK. They are:

1. The strong pound

From 1992 to 2008 the value of pound rose significantly. This put downward pressure on the price of imports, meaning that overall price increases of goods in particular, were restrained. A stronger pound reduced the price of services and finished goods, but also lowered the price of raw materials used to make products in the UK. The UK is a relatively open economy with the value of imports exceeding 30% of GDP. Therefore, lower import prices due to a strong pound had a significant effect. Even on the eve of the Brexit vote in June 2016 the pound was relatively strong, with many arguing that Sterling had been overvalued for many years.

2. Exogenous shocks

During the 1970s there were a number of hikes in the price of essential sources of energy. The price of oil rose from under $5 per barrel in 1970 to over $25 by 1980. This was a major contributing factor to a period of stagflation (high unemployment and high inflation) in the UK at that time. The period 1992-2007 however, saw no major exogenous shocks, and commodity prices remained reasonably stable which kept cost-push inflationary pressures in check. Despite oil price spikes in 2008 and 2011, where the price of a barrel of oil exceeded $145 per barrel, monthly inflation only temporarily topped 5% in those years, as shown in Figure 8.9. In fact the price of commodities, such as oil, fell dramatically from the summer of 2014 as shown in Figure 8.10, and this contributed to the low rates of inflation that followed in 2015 and 2016.

A combination of a slowdown in the growth rate of emerging markets, especially China, and an increase in global oil production through fracking, particularly in the US, caused a collapse in global oil prices. Falling

Figure 8.9: UK monthly CPI inflation (%) 2006-2016

Source: ONS

Figure 8.10: Brent crude oil price 2006-2016,
US$ per barrel

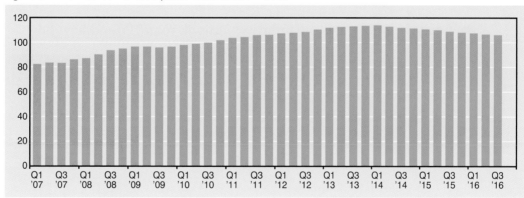

Source: OTC

oil and commodity prices fell through to lower production costs, putting downward pressure on the price of many basic goods such as food, which saw price falls during 2015 and 2016, as shown in Figure 8.11. This fed through to negative goods price inflation, as shown in Figure 8.3, reducing overall CPI inflation to a 0% in 2015, with inflation remaining low throughout 2016.

Figure 8.11: UK consumer food prices index (2010 = 100)

Source: OECD

3. Competitive product markets

(i) Domestic factors: The 1980s and 1990s saw a period of privatisation and deregulation. This led to greater competition, especially in the utility sector, which put downward pressure on prices. Furthermore, a tougher approach towards competition policy was adopted. The Competition Act of 1998 saw the Competition Commission replacing the Monopolies and Mergers Commission, and the 2002 Enterprise Act gave the new Commission far more power than its predecessor. The effect was to encourage competition across many sectors which put downward pressure on inflation. The Office of Fair Trading and the Competition Commission were merged to form the Competition and Markets Authority in 2014 to give the competition authorities real 'teeth', further improving the competitiveness of domestic markets, putting downward pressure on prices.

(ii) Global factors: During this period many countries joined the WTO and the global economy more generally. The UK faced rising competition from newly-industrialised countries (NICs) such as from China, India and countries in Eastern Europe. These countries have much lower unit labour costs, and thus have a comparative advantage in labour-intensive industries. As a result, UK manufacturers faced stiff competition from overseas and were forced to reduce mark-ups and costs. This effect, along with greater import volumes of goods from NICs, put downward pressure on the price of basic manufactures such as clothing, footwear, and household items.

4. Flexible labour markets

Three factors made the UK's Labour market more flexible during this period:

(i) Greater female participation in the workforce increased the supply of labour and reduced wage-inflationary pressures.

(ii) Significant immigration from outside and inside the EU increased the supply of labour and helped to plug skills shortages in certain industries. On 1st January 2004 ten new countries, mostly from Central and Eastern Europe, joined the EU. Afterwards a significant influx of self-selecting, productive workers came to the UK.

(iii) Since the 1980s there has been a significant amount of 'de-unionisation' in the UK, partly due to government policy in the 1980s, and partly due to the relative decline of the more unionised manufacturing sector. Wage bargaining power has declined as a result, reducing cost-push inflationary pressures.

5. Credible monetary policy

After being tasked with controlling inflation in 1998, the Bank of England acted quickly when there were signs of growing inflationary pressure by raising interest rates. Such pre-emptive action and a clearly defined policy framework helped to build faith in the Bank of England's ability to keep inflation within the 1-3% acceptable boundary. This helped to lower **inflationary expectations**, and thus wage demands remained subdued during this period.

● Analysis: **Brexit and the inflation outlook for 2017 and beyond**

The vote to leave the EU on 23rd June 2016 has made macroeconomic forecasting extremely difficult. Prior to the referendum the majority of economists believed that a vote to leave the EU would harm the UK economy in the short term. In May 2016 David Cameron, the then Prime Minister, and George Osborne, Chancellor of the Exchequer, warned that the UK would slip into a DIY 'Brexit recession' if the UK voted to leave the EU. However, in the months immediately following the referendum the economy continued to grow, and consumer confidence remained buoyant. One major fear was that investment, and inward foreign direct investment in particular, would decline sharply due to uncertainty over the UK's future trading arrangements and growth prospects. However, following the vote to leave the EU several major companies, including Nissan and Jaguar Land Rover have said that they would be increasing their investment in the UK. So, while the outlook for growth and employment is very much up for debate, there is much more of a consensus of what Brexit means for inflation.

Following the vote to leave the EU several major companies, including Nissan and Jaguar Land Rover have said that they would be increasing their investment in the UK.

Figure 8.12: Sterling exchange rates

Source: Bank of England, November 2016 Inflation Report

Figure 8.13: CPI inflation projection based on constant nominal interest rates at 0.25%, other policy measures as announced

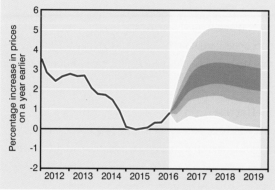

Source: Bank of England, November 2016 Inflation Report

Figures 8.12 shows how the value of the pound collapsed following the Brexit vote, and has remained low. As the value of imports to the UK exceeds 30% of GDP, the rise in import prices will have a significant effect on the overall rate of inflation. The price of clothes and electronics, most of which are imported, are set to rise sharply. Furthermore, as the price of oil and other commodity prices are denominated in US dollars, the Sterling price of oil and other imported commodities is set to rise sharply, putting upward pressure on the price of many goods including basic staples such as food. Former Sainsbury's chief Justin King warned of a 5% rise in food prices through 2017. Figure 8.13 shows that the Bank of England expects inflation to rise sharply in 2017 before peaking in 2018, and most economic forecasts show a similar trend.

In the fan chart, the darker the shade, the more likely the rate of inflation according to the Bank's own forecasts. So even though there is a strong chance of a sharp rise in inflation in 2017, there is clearly a degree of uncertainty over the outlook for inflation, and most major macroeconomic variables following the UK's vote to leave the EU.

Since the Great Recession of 2008, nominal wage growth has been very sluggish, often exceeded by the rate of inflation, meaning that real incomes and therefore living standards have been squeezed (see Chapter 4). The return of higher inflation following the Brexit vote means that after a brief period of rising real wages, the 'squeeze' on living standards is set to continue. In November 2016 the reputable Institute for Fiscal Studies predicted that by 2021 workers would earn less in real wages that in 2008. Despite the predicted rise in inflation, it will not be caused by real income growth fuelling demand-pull pressures.

Extension material: 'Core' inflation

A measure of 'core' inflation can be useful as it excludes price changes in volatile items such as food and energy. Therefore, it is a reasonable measure of 'underlying' inflationary pressure in the economy. However, as high commodity prices could be a more frequent feature than during the NICE decade, cost-push, rather than demand-pull pressures might well be the main cause of inflation for several years to come. 'Core' inflation therefore, might not be a very good predictor of actual changes in the rate of inflation.

● Knowledge: **Deflation**

Deflation is a sustained **fall** in the general price level. It is important to distinguish between deflation which may be harmful, and deflation that does not harm macroeconomic performance.

(i) Deflation may occur due to technological advances and productivity gains that cause long-run economic growth. As the long-run aggregate supply curve shifts to the right, there is downward pressure on the price level. This is known as *benign* deflation.

(ii) However, a lack of aggregate demand may also cause the overall price level to fall. This has been a persistent problem in Japan since the 1990s, as shown in Figures 8.7 and 8.8. This type is known as *malign* deflation. Since the global recession of 2008-09 the European Central Bank and other policy makers have feared that the Eurozone may be headed for a period of Japanese-style deflation, and have taken unprecedented steps to try to avoid it. This danger loomed large in September 2014, with Eurozone inflation falling to just 0.3%.

● Analysis: **Reasons why malign deflation damages macroeconomic performance**

There are several reasons why deflation due to a lack of aggregate demand is a problem:

1. Deferred consumption

If consumers see prices falling today, they will postpone consumption as prices will be lower in the future. Therefore, consumption and aggregate demand will fall, reducing growth and employment. The resulting fall in the price level further entrenches the deflation problem.

2. Rising real value of debt

As prices fall, nominal wages may fall as well. Employers may try to justify cuts in nominal wages when prices are falling. In addition, as aggregate demand in the economy is weak, workers are in a weak bargaining position. As nominal wages fall, it becomes harder for households to repay their debts, as their nominal value remains unchanged. This means that households must allocate a greater proportion of income towards debt repayment, and cut back on consumption.

3. Monetary policy becomes ineffective

Deflation can cause monetary policy to become a significantly less powerful policy instrument. To try to boost aggregate demand and prevent a persistent period of deflation from occurring, a central bank will cut interest rates. However, if interest rates are cut by 1%, but prices fall by 2%, the **real interest rate** has actually risen, which encourages saving and discourages consumer spending. Moreover, once interest rates have been cut to zero, there is nothing more that interest changes can do to boost aggregate demand, thus rendering interest rate cuts ineffective, and central banks will have to resort to printing money (quantitative easing), as is the policy in Japan and the Eurozone today.

4. Large fiscal deficits and debt burdens emerge

As monetary policy becomes ineffective in stimulating aggregate demand, the government must adopt an expansionary fiscal policy instead. A sustained budget deficit could lead to excessive levels of national debt being accumulated, which will create a drag on growth in the long term. This is what happened in Japan, where national debt reached 227% of GDP by 2014.

Essay Questions

5. Examine the effects of a rise in the price of oil upon UK macroeconomic performance.
6. Evaluate the view that adjusting interest rates is the best way to manage the rate of inflation in the UK.
7. "Deflation is always bad for macroeconomic performance." To what extent do you agree with this statement?

Chapter 9

Monetary Policy in the UK

Monetary policy is defined as government policy regarding interest rates, exchange rates and the money supply. Since 1992 the UK has had a floating exchange rate, and thus the value of the pound is not deliberately altered by policy makers. Until recently monetary policy in effect meant the setting of interest rates, but in 2009 the Bank of England started to use a new policy; **quantitative easing**. The Monetary Policy Committee at the Bank of England are the focal point of this chapter; the committee members themselves, the tools they use to target inflation, and how successful they have been in achieving their objective.

● ● Knowledge and Application: The UK monetary policy framework

On 6th May 1997 the newly-elected government announced plans to give the Bank of England independence, which was achieved under the 1998 Bank of England Act. The Monetary Policy Committee (MPC) at the Bank of England was given operational independence for setting interest rates to achieve **price stability**, while supporting the government's targets for growth and employment. Those in favour of independence argued that by being free of political interference, the Bank of England should gain credibility for controlling inflation. The MPC contains 9 members.

The MPC's task is to achieve the inflation target by adjusting the base rate. The base rate (also known as the repo rate) is the interest rate at which the Bank of England lends to commercial banks. Since 2003 the Bank of England has had an inflation target of 2.0% on the CPI measure, with a symmetrical 'acceptable boundary' of between 1 and 3%.

Figure 9.1: Bank of England base rate (%) 1999-2016

Source: Bank of England

It takes up to two years for the full effect of a change in the interest rate to have its impact upon aggregate demand and therefore inflation. As a result, the MPC makes interest rate decisions to try to achieve the inflation target in two years time, and therefore acts in a *pre-emptive* manner, rather than in response to recent changes in the inflation rate. The MPC gathers information to predict inflation into the future, and adjust the base rate to try to bring future inflation back to target. One good example of the pre-emptive setting of the interest rate came in late 2008. The Bank of England cut the base rate from 4.5% to 0.5% between October 2008 and March 2009 despite the fact that inflation remained above target throughout this period. In fact, when the base rate was cut on 4th October 2008 the previous month's CPI inflation rate was 5.2%, the highest level since 1992. The MPC was cutting rates as they predicted a fall in core inflationary pressure as the economy fell into recession.

The MPC meets for one and a half days, eight times a year, to decide the Bank of England Base Rate of interest in the United Kingdom. Members hear a wealth of data on the domestic and global economy from Bank of England economists and regional representatives. The data includes developments in trade, investment, financial markets, productivity, the budget balance and many other indicators. Ultimately the Bank is trying to decide how strong domestic demand will be relative to the productive capacity of the economy, in effect, predicting the future output gap. If domestic demand is growing faster than the economy's productive potential then inflationary pressure will be forecast to grow, and interest rates should be raised.

On the basis of the data the MPC members must decide if inflation is set to hit the target in two years time. Members then vote on whether to hold, raise, or cut the base rate. Each member has one vote, and the majority decision is implemented.

There were disagreements between MPC members over base rate changes in August and September 2014 for the first time since July 2011. In spite of very weak wage growth through 2013 and 2014, Ian McCafferty and Martin Weale expected a sharp rise in wage inflation as unemployment fell below 6% and the UK economy would start to run up against capacity constraints. The pair voted in favour of a 0.25% rise in the base rate but the other seven members of the MPC including Mark Carney, the Governor of the Bank of England, voted in favour of holding the base rate at 0.5% citing a benign inflationary outlook. Since the end of the recession in 2009 there was

Mark Carney, Governor of the Bank of England.

ongoing speculation as to when interest rates would start going up. Mark Carney promised that when base rate rises were made they they would be "gradual and limited", but the first change in the base rate of interest since March 2009 came in August 2016 following the Brexit vote, when Mark Carney announced that the base rate of interest would be cut to just 0.25% to help the economy through a period of uncertainty. The MPC unanimously voted for the base rate cut to 0.25%.

Questions

1. The Monetary Policy Committee (MPC) is most likely to raise interest rates if:
   A. Unemployment is rising.
   B. The exchange rate is appreciating.
   C. The growth of the money supply is decreasing.
   D. Domestic demand is set to rise above the level of potential GDP.

2. Explain the difficulty in measuring the size of an output gap.

Due to the important role of expectations, monetary policy is most likely to be successful if the Bank of England has *credibility*. That is, the public believe in the MPC's ability to control inflation. A number of measures have been used to try to achieve this:

(i) The workings of the MPC are **transparent**, and members are accountable. The minutes of the meeting are published soon after the meeting, and show how each member voted. Those in the minority are asked to state the action they would have preferred.

(ii) Members of the MPC regularly appear before parliamentary committees, usually the **Treasury Select Committee**, to answer questions about their decisions. The MPC is also accountable to the **Court of the Bank**, comprising experts in commerce, industry and finance.

(iii) If the rate of inflation goes outside of the 1-3% 'acceptable' limits the Governor of the Bank of England must write an **open letter** to the Chancellor of the Exchequer to explain why the inflation target has been missed, and how he/she intends to rectify this.

(iv) The **Inflation Report**, published each quarter, provides details on recent developments in the economy and monetary policy, justifying the MPC's actions.

(v) Perhaps most importantly, the MPC is made up of **experts from a wide variety of backgrounds** including academics, monetary policy experts and economists from industry.

The 9 members of the Monetary Policy Committee (November 2016)

Mark Carney	Governor of the Bank of England
Ben Broadbent	Deputy Governor (responsible for Monetary Policy)
Sir Jon Cunliffe	Deputy Governor (responsible for Financial Stability)
Nemat Shafik	Deputy Governor (responsible for Markets and Banking)
Andy Haldane	Executive Director, Monetary Analysis & Chief Economist
Kristin Forbes	External member, Professor of Management and Global Economics at MIT
Michael Saunders	External member, former Head of European Economics at Citigroup
Ian McCafferty	External member, former Chief Economic Adviser to the CBI
Gertjan Vlieghe	External member, former senior economist at Brevan Howard Asset Management

● Analysis: Why does the UK have an inflation target?

There are several advantages from having a specific 2.0% inflation target:

1. Reducing inflationary expectations

By having a *credible* 2.0% target, workers will moderate their wage claims accordingly, as they can achieve real income growth without large pay demands. This reduces cost-push inflationary pressures. Similarly, businesses will avoid large price increases if prices across the economy are not expected to rise significantly.

2. Failure of targeting 'intermediate variables'

Intermediate variables (i.e. variables which influence the rate of inflation such as the exchange rate or the money supply) can be targeted rather than inflation itself. During the 1980s there was no specific inflation target. Instead, the Thatcher government tried, unsuccessfully, to control the money supply, which continued to grow. Targeting inflation directly allows policy-makers to consider **all** the factors that influence inflation, rather than fixating on one or two.

3. Keeping fiat money credible

The value of money is no longer tied to gold. Instead, *fiat* money is only worth something because people believe it has value, and one of the most important jobs of any government is to preserve the value of money. Therefore, it is beneficial to have a monetary policy framework which protects against inflation and helps people to believe that their money will have almost the same worth tomorrow as today.

4. Success of inflation targeting elsewhere

Inflation targeting has proved effective in other countries, particularly in New Zealand and Canada after they adopted the policy in the early 1990s.

● Analysis: The transmission mechanism of monetary policy

Changes in interest rates affect inflation primarily through their impact on aggregate demand, and also through changes in the price of imported goods and services. A fall in interest rates, such as the fall in the base rate from 5.0% to 0.5% between April 2008 and March 2009 could impact upon the economy via a number of channels:

1. Household saving and borrowing

Lower interest rates reduce the cost of borrowing, and reduce the return on saving. This should raise the level of borrowing and reduce the savings ratio, thus increasing consumption and aggregate demand. Demand for consumer durables (e.g. cars, computers) should rise significantly, as they are usually purchased on credit.

2. Mortgage repayments and effective disposable income

According to the Financial Services Authority (FSA) around 70% of mortgages in the UK are variable rate mortgages. Therefore, a fall in the interest rate will mean that monthly mortgage repayments will fall, increasing the effective disposable income of homeowners. This should boost consumption and hence aggregate demand. This effect is especially significant for the UK, as around 67% of households were 'owner-occupied' in 2012, far higher than most of Europe.

3. Asset prices and the 'wealth effect'

As interest rates fall, the return on holding cash savings accounts diminishes. Therefore savers and investors in search of a better return are more likely to purchase equities or property, thus increasing their demand and value. Furthermore, more people will be tempted to buy property when interest rates are low, as mortgage payments will be lower. This puts further upward pressure on property prices. As asset prices rise, people see their wealth value increase and 'feel' richer, boosting consumer confidence and consumption. In addition, some households will take out loans against the rising value of their properties, adding to consumption. This is known as **equity withdrawal**.

4. Investment and the 'hurdle rate'

At any point in time firms have a number of potential investment projects. The hurdle rate is the minimum expected return a company demands before it goes ahead with a project given the risks involved. Many investments are funded through borrowing. As interest rates fall, the expected return of a project rises as the cost of the project has fallen. Therefore more projects become profitable, so more will go ahead, thus increasing overall investment and aggregate demand.

5. The exchange rate, net exports and import prices

As interest rates fall, there is a 'hot money' outflow as international investors see a fall on their return from keeping money in UK banks. This causes demand for the pound to fall, resulting in currency depreciation. As a result exports become more attractive while imports become more expensive, resulting in a rise in net exports, aggregate demand, and inflation. Furthermore, a rise in the price of imports directly raises the price level.

Figure 9.2: The monetary policy transmission mechanism

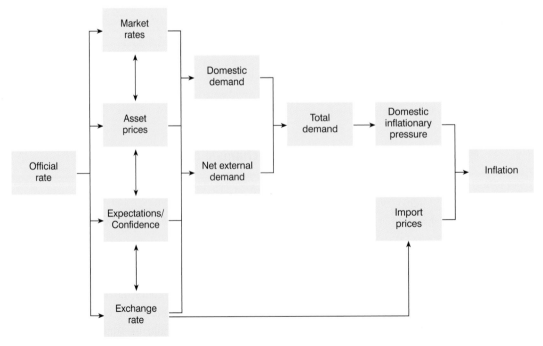

Source: Bank of England

● Evaluation: The effects of a fall in interest rates

Making accurate forecasts over the impact of a fall in interest rates is difficult for several reasons:

1. **Time lags** – Commercial banks do not immediately adjust their retail interest rates in response to a fall in the base rate, and it takes a further year for the full impact of a change in aggregate demand to affect inflation.

2. **Asymmetric impact on households** – Individuals who rely heavily on savings (e.g. pensioners) will see their income from interest fall in response to a fall in the base rate, and thus their spending may fall. However, this effect is outweighed by higher borrowing, less saving and more spending from most households, increasing aggregate demand overall.

3. **Asymmetric impact on firms** – When interest rates fall some firms will see their income from cash deposits fall, potentially reducing their level of investment. However, across all firms, lower interest rates tend to boost investment levels due to the lower cost of borrowing to finance investment projects.

4. **Some mortgages are fixed rate** – some mortgages in the UK offer fixed rates of interest, and thus monthly repayments will not fall in response to a base rate cut until the term of the fixed rate expires, and the terms of the mortgage are renegotiated. However, most mortgages in the UK are 'variable rate'.

Figure 9.3: Bank Rate and quoted interest rates on new household borrowing following the Great Recession

Source: Bank of England

5. **De-coupling** – When the Bank of England cut the base rate dramatically between late 2008 and early 2009, rates on key personal loans such as credit cards and overdrafts actually increased as shown in Figure 9.3. This was due to banks trying to repair their balance sheets in the wake of the financial crisis, higher interbank lending rates and the banks attaching a higher 'risk premium' to lending during a time of recession and enormous uncertainty.

6. **Willingness to borrow/lend** – Despite the significant base rate cuts between late 2008 and early 2009, the savings rate rose considerably due to falling consumer confidence, and households became less willing to borrow as consumers prepared for a 'rainy day'. Simultaneously, banks became less willing to lend, which harmed SMEs who struggled to access much needed credit.

● Evaluation: How well has the UK monetary policy framework worked?

Since the Bank of England was granted control of the base rate of interest with the objective of controlling inflation in 1997, most would argue that the effect has been broadly positive, especially in the first 10 years. There are several reasons for this:

● From Bank of England independence in May 1997 right through to March 2007 monthly CPI inflation was within the target range the vast majority of the time.

● The MPC were praised by the House of Commons Treasury Select Committee for establishing a credible inflation targeting record.

● The UK's inflation performance was stronger than most of her European and North American competitors between 1997 and 2007.

Figure 9.4: UK CPI and Bank of England Base Rate, 1999-2016

Source:ONS, Bank of England

- The Bank of England was effective in pre-empting future inflationary pressure and taking action as demonstrated by repeated rate rises in early 2004, when the MPC lifted the bank rate by a full percentage point which caused inflation to fall back to target by the end of 2005.

- In 1997 Bank of England Governor Mervyn King acknowledged the Bank of England's role in supporting other macroeconomic objectives, particularly growth and employment. He stated that central bankers should not be 'inflation nutters' i.e. they should not focus purely on controlling inflation at the expense of growth and employment, a popular criticism of the European Central Bank (ECB). The MPC's significant base rate cuts in 2001 were effective in preventing a major downturn, and in 2008 the Bank cut the base rate to support growth and employment despite the fact that inflation at the time was well above target.

However, there has also been some criticism of the MPC, which has grown since 2007:

- The UK's inflation performance worsened considerably after the beginning of the financial crisis in the autumn of 2007, both relative to the UK's main competitors and in relation to the inflation target. Between September 2007 and September 2012 CPI inflation was above the 3% upper acceptable boundary for 40 out of 60 months. During this time Mervyn King had to write 14 open letters to the Chancellor explaining why the MPC failed to keep inflation within the 1-3% boundary, whereas no letters were written during the previous 10 years.

- Some argue that the MPC has not always reacted quickly enough to changes in inflationary pressure. Inflationary pressure started to rise from the beginning of 2006 but the MPC did not raise the base rate until August of that year. More significant however, was the MPC's late reaction in cutting interest rates as the UK economy fell into a deep recession in 2008. GDP had been falling since the second quarter of 2008, but inflation reached 5.2% in September of that year largely due to a temporary commodity price spike. Critics argue that the MPC should have recognised that these pressures were temporary, and that underlying inflationary pressure at the time was falling dramatically due to collapsing demand and rising unemployment. The Bank of England cut the base rate aggressively from 5.0% in October 2008 to 0.5% in March 2009, but this was not enough to stop CPI inflation falling well below target, and the RPI measure showed a period of deflation for much of 2009.

- Some believe that the MPC's objectives have become blurred in recent years, thus eroding their credibility for inflation targeting. Critics argue that since the 2008-09 recession more emphasis has been put on growth rather than targeting inflation. During 2010 inflationary pressure grew significantly, and CPI inflation averaged 4.5% in 2011. Yet the Bank of England did not raise interest rates, keeping the base rate at the historic low of 0.5%. The fact that the UK economy narrowly avoided falling back into recession in 2011 and 2012 suggests that the Bank of England sided with supporting growth rather than controlling inflation. Supporters of the MPC are quick to point out that much of this inflation was due to temporary factors beyond their control (such as the VAT rise to 20% and energy price increases) and that underlying pressures remained weak. Inflation did fall back to below 3% by May 2012 and continued to fall through 2013 to reach just 1.2% in September 2014, which supports the view that interest rates should have remained at their historical low. To bring some clarity to the Bank of England's position on supporting growth and employment Mark Carney, the new Governor of the Bank of England from July 2013 announced some explicit 'forward guidance' on the conduct of future monetary policy (see below) just one month after taking up his position.

- Critics have argued that monetary policy has been operating under a 'one tool, one target' framework which has focussed too much on targeting overall price increases while ignoring the impact of policy instruments on key asset prices such as house prices. Although monetary policy was effective in controlling overall price increases during the NICE decade (1997-2007), double digit house price inflation was the norm. In the UK and the US an extended period of low interest rates and high credit availability, especially in the early 2000s, fuelled a house price bubble which may have boosted consumer confidence and prevented deflation in the short term, but increased the risk of deflation when the housing bubble burst in 2007-8. In the wake of the financial crisis of 2008 there has been a consensus amongst economists that central banks should do more to prevent excessive lending and asset bubbles emerging in order to reduce the risk they pose to financial stability. The Financial Services Act 2012, which came into force in April 2013, was a direct response to this. It established an independent Financial Policy Committee (FPC), a new prudential regulator as a subsidiary of the Bank, and created new responsibilities for the supervision of financial market infrastructure. The (FPC) contributes to the achievement of the Bank's financial stability objective. It is charged with taking action to remove or reduce systemic risks with a view to protecting and enhancing the resilience of the UK financial system.

Recent changes to the policy framework: Forward guidance

Through 2010 and 2011 inflation was above the 'acceptable' upper boundary of 3% every month but the Bank kept the base rate at 0.5%. This was partly due to the fact that the inflationary pressure was largely due to 'cost-push' factors such as rising global food, energy and other commodity prices which are beyond the control of the MPC, but it became clear that the Bank of England was clearly intent on supporting growth and employment during the faltering recovery. Critics said that the Bank's objectives had become blurred, and ill-defined. To deal with this the MPC voted to provide some explicit 'forward guidance' on the future conduct of monetary policy at its meeting on 1st August 2013. The MPC said it intended to maintain an expansive monetary policy, continuing with a record low base rate and asset purchases (quantitative easing, see below) until 'economic slack' had been substantially reduced, provided this did not entail material risks to either price stability or financial stability. In particular, the MPC said it intended not to raise the Bank Rate from 0.5% at least until the unemployment rate fell to a threshold of 7%, subject to the conditions below. The guidance linking Bank Rate and asset sales to the unemployment threshold would cease to hold if any of the following three 'knockouts' were breached:

1. In the MPC's view, it became more likely than not, that CPI inflation 18 to 24 months ahead would be 0.5 percentage points or more above the 2% target.

2. Medium-term inflation expectations no longer remained sufficiently well anchored.

3. The Financial Policy Committee (FPC) judged that the stance of monetary policy posed a significant threat to financial stability (e.g. the emergence of asset bubbles) that could not be contained by the range of policy actions available to the FPC, the Financial Conduct Authority and the Prudential Regulation Authority.

The unemployment rate fell below 7% in February 2014 yet the Bank of England did not raise the base rate due to falling inflationary pressure and a benign inflationary outlook. This approach appeared to be the correct course of action as both inflation and unemployment continued to fall into 2015, with inflation falling below 0% and unemployment falling below 5%, and both inflation and unemployment remained at similar levels through 2016.

Quantitative easing

By March 2009 the base rate had been cut to a historic low of 0.5% in an attempt to boost aggregate demand, but the UK economy remained in a deep recession and there was a continued threat of deflation. As a result, the MPC decided to try something new; **Quantitative Easing (QE)**.

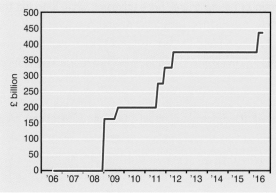

Figure 9.5: UK Asset Purchase Facility (£bn)

Source: Bank of England

As shown in Figure 9.5, by late 2012 £375bn had been created electronically by the Bank of England and placed into an 'Asset Purchase Facility'. This money is then used to buy illiquid assets, mostly government bonds, from financial institutions in exchange for more liquid cash. As a result, financial institutions have more loanable funds which can be passed onto households and firms, thus boosting aggregate demand, and putting upward pressure on prices. As the Bank of England is a big buyer in the bonds ('gilts') market, higher demand for bonds increases their price, reducing the yields and effective interest rates on bonds, which are the benchmark for some mortgage rates, bank overdraft rates and business borrowing rates. This should encourage borrowing and spending. Crucially, the Bank of England uses the newly-created money to purchase gilts from private investors such as pension funds and insurance companies. These investors typically do not want to hold on to this money, because it yields a low return. So they tend to use it to purchase other assets, such as corporate bonds and shares. That lowers longer-term borrowing costs and encourages the issuance of new equities and bonds, as well as increasing asset prices, confidence and overall spending in the economy.

Arguments in favour of quantitative easing

1. The supply of credit should increase due to greater liquidity in the financial system, as should the demand for credit due to lower interest rates. This should boost aggregate demand and put upward pressure on prices, thus reducing deflationary risks.

2. The Bank of England base rate cannot be lowered much further, thus new policy instruments are needed.

3. The policy could stimulate lending more directly than a base rate cut due to its direct impact on several benchmark lending rates.

4. The policy may have prevented recession and a descent into a deflationary spiral in Japan between 2001 and 2006.

Arguments against quantitative easing

1. Inflationary pressure

A significant rise in the money supply always poses the risk of causing inflation, as too much money chasing goods and services will lead to inflation. Milton Friedman famously said 'inflation is always and everywhere

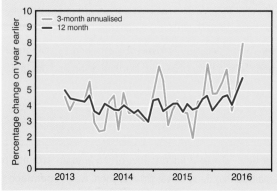

Figure 9.6: M4 seasonally-adjusted money supply excluding intermediate OFCs

Source: Bank of England

a monetary phenomenom'. Initially, following the Great Recession, injecting more money into a dwindling effective money supply, as shown in Figure 9.6, seemed to make sense as preventing a fall in the money supply was directly combating deflationary pressures. However, if money supply growth exceeds nominal GDP growth, a rise in the price of goods and services and/or assets, is likely. As Figure 9.6 shows, the growth of the money supply accelerated through 2015 and 2016, while the Bank announced an additional £60bn in asset purchases. The Bank argued this was necessary to support the economy in a time of uncertainty following the Brexit vote, and help the Bank to achieve it's sustainable 2% inflation target, but some economists thought this may 'add fuel to the fire', adding to inflationary pressure, or asset price bubbles.

2. Blurred objectives

Critics have argued that elements of the QE policy are a sign that the Bank of England has become blurred in their objectives. Many argue that an unstated goal of QE is to help the ailing financial system to recover from the financial crisis by injecting much needed liquidity, which should prevent financial institutions from collapsing and guard against risks posed from potential default by Eurozone governments. In addition, many claim another unstated goal of QE is to help the UK government borrow at reduced rates of interest, which is particularly important given the large size of the budget deficit since the 2008-09 recession. Finally, some argue that elements of the QE policy show that the Bank of England has become more focussed on boosting growth rather than controlling inflation. For example, the MPC announced the creation of a further £75bn to be injected into the economy in October 2011, at a time when inflation was well above target at 5.0%.

3. Is QE reaching consumers and businesses?

Since the asset purchase programme was extended beyond the initial £200bn in October 2010, the amount of liquid money on banks' balance sheets has risen by around 58% but loans issued to households and businesses has remained almost unchanged. This suggests that banks are holding onto this extra liquidity to improve their balance sheets, rather than increasing their lending, as the policy aimed to. The fear is that when macroeconomic conditions improve and confidence returns, banks could increase lending significantly, thus increasingly the effective money supply and inflation. However, the Bank of England could reverse the QE process and sell bonds back to the market if it looks like inflation may go above target.

4. Wealth inequality and asset bubbles

There is strong evidence that QE has added substantially to wealth inequality. The policy deliberately aims to increase asset prices. Wealthier households own more assets such as houses and shares, and thus they gain far more from pumped up asset prices than less wealthy households. There is also the fear that QE is simply contributing to asset bubbles, particularly in the housing market, as QE puts downward pressure on interest rates making riskier investments in shares and property more appealing.

5. Limits to the effectiveness of QE

Towards the end of 2012 Mervyn King acknowledged that QE might be reaching the limit of its effectiveness. On 1st August 2012 the Treasury and the Bank of England launched the **Funding for Lending** bank scheme, where commercial banks can borrow from the Bank of England at low rates of interest (just 0.75%) on the condition that they increase lending to households and small businesses, with penalties if this was not achieved. In its early stages, the scheme was broadly deemed to be a success. The **Term Funding Scheme** (**TFS**) introduced in August 2016 had a similar objective, rewarding financial institutions that passed on the cut in the base rate to businesses and consumers in the real economy. Thus, the risk of 'de-coupling' should be reduced.

6. Are financial markets addicted to QE?

In theory, the QE process was always temporary, and all bonds purchased by the Bank of England should be sold back to financial markets in a reverse of the process when normal economic conditions are restored. This would take liquidity out of the financial system and reduce inflationary risks during an upturn. However, such a reversal of the process remains a very distant prospect, as even the suggestion of 'tapering' QE, as suggested by Ben Bernanke, the then Chairman of the Federal Reserve in the US, sent financial markets into a 'tantrum' in 2013. The price of shares, property and other assets are artificially high as a result of QE, and any attempt to reverse the process will not come without asset prices being negatively affected, and falling asset prices will impact negatively on growth.

Extension material: The relationship between money supply (M4) and inflation

M4 is a measure of the broad money supply in the economy and is often driven by bank lending. The general relationship between the money supply and the price level is a proportional one, as stated by the famous monetarist Milton Friedman when he stated that 'inflation is always and everywhere a monetary phenomenon'. The Fisher equation supports this view: $MV = PT$ where M = money supply, V = velocity of circulation, P = price level and T = number of transactions or real output. If V and T remain constant, which is not unrealistic in the short run, a rise in the money supply should directly lead to a rise in the price level. However, V has varied considerably in recent years. Since 2008-09, low consumer and business confidence due to macroeconomic uncertainty caused agents to hold onto their money for longer as they are less willing to spend.

Figure 9.7: M4 broad money, credit, and Nominal GDP

Source: Bank of England; *M4 and M4 lending (excluding securitisations) growth prior to 1998 Q4, and equivalent measures excluding the deposits of, and borrowing by, intermediate OFCs thereafter; †M4 excluding intermediate other financial corporations (OFCs); ‡At current market prices (real GDP).

If broad money growth exceeds nominal GDP growth (the rise in the value of output of goods and services) you would expect significant inflation to be the result, as there would be more money chasing goods and services, thus 'bidding up' their prices. However, as shown in Figure 9.7 broad money growth was considerably higher than nominal GDP growth for much of 2000-2008, without causing significant inflation. There are a few possible explanations for this: money, especially consumer credit, was being used to purchase large quantities of foreign goods; large quantities of money were being used to buy assets which raised asset price (e.g. housing price) inflation but not wider inflation; broad money growth during this period was concentrated in the hands of OFCs (Other Financial Corporations) such as pension and private equity funds, who do not spend lots of money in the conventional sense; and lastly money may have been borrowed in the UK, adding to the money supply figures but spent on assets abroad.

There was a rapid fall in broad money growth from 2008 onwards, largely due to the Credit Crunch, where banks reduced lending considerably. The rapid fall in money supply growth in 2008-09 was a major cause of inflation falling below target by June 2009, and the threat of deflation became very real. This was a major justification for Quantitative Easing, which aimed to boost the money supply and reduce the risk of deflation. The £125bn of asset purchases made by the Bank of England in the nine months to June 2012 were a major factor in bringing about a rise in money supply growth in 2012. However, nominal GDP only rose by £30bn, providing more evidence that commercial banks were not passing on the money received from their sale of bonds to the Bank of England. This highlights the fact that the relationship between the money supply and inflation is far from straightforward.

Questions

3. Explain how quantitative easing can be used to prevent deflation.

4. 'The Bank of England has been very successful in controlling inflation since being given independence in 1997'. To what extent do you agree with this statement?

Chapter 10

UK Fiscal Policy

In this chapter we explore recent changes to tax rates and trends in government expenditure under the Labour, Coalition and Conservative governments.

● Knowledge: **Defining fiscal policy**

Fiscal policy is government policy regarding taxation, government spending and borrowing. It is primarily a demand-management policy used to influence macroeconomic variables such as aggregate demand, but it can also be used to influence the supply side of the economy, and it also has a large microeconomic impact as it addresses market failures.

There are several objectives of fiscal policy:

1. To manage demand in the economy.

2. To fund government spending.

3. To correct market failures, such as the problem of public goods and externalities.

4. To redistribute income and wealth.

5. To improve the supply side performance of the economy.

● Knowledge: **Types of taxation**

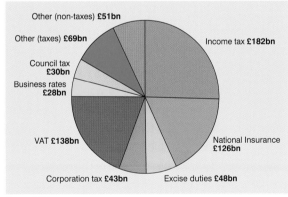

Figure 10.1: Sources of public sector receipts (tax revenue) 2016-17, £bn

Source: OBR

Total tax revenue for the 2016-17 financial year is expected to be £716bn. Business rates and Council Tax are collected by local authorities, but the majority of taxes are collected by HM Revenue and Customs.

Direct taxes are taxes levied directly on an individual or organisation, such as income tax, corporation tax or national insurance contributions (NICs). As shown by Figure 10.1, income tax is the most important contributor to government revenue, followed by VAT and NICs. Direct taxes tend to be **progressive**, where a higher proportion of income is paid in tax as the income level increases.

Indirect taxes are taxes levied on goods and services, effectively taxing expenditure. Figure 10.1 shows that Value Added Tax (VAT) is the most important source of indirect tax revenue. Other indirect taxes include excise duties, air passenger duty, customs duties and landfill tax. Unlike direct taxes, the burden of the tax can be passed onto a third party. VAT, for example, is levied on the producer, but they can choose to pass some of the burden of the tax onto the consumer. Indirect taxes tend to be **regressive**, where a higher proportion of income is paid in tax as the income level falls.

● Application: **Changes in UK tax rates**

Table 10.1 shows a shift in the burden of taxation away from direct taxes such as income tax, towards higher indirect taxes such as VAT. Much of this shift occurred under the Conservative Government 1979-1997. Such a shift is controversial, as it made the tax system less progressive overall. This is partly responsible for the significant rise in the level of income inequality under the Conservatives, as explained in Chapter 4.

Table 10.1: Changes in UK income tax and VAT rates

| Year | Income tax rates (%) | | | | VAT rate (%) |
	Starting rate	Basic	Higher	New Top Rate	Standard rate
1978					8
1979	-	33	83	-	15
1988	-	25	40	-	
1991					17.5
1992	25	25	40	-	
1997	20	24	40	-	
1999	10	22	40	-	
2008	-	20	40	-	15
2010	-	20	40	50	17.5
2011					20
2013	-	20	40	45	20
2014	-	20	40	45	20
2015	-	20	40	45	20
2016	-	20	40	45	20

● Analysis: **Income tax and tax credits**

The reason for the cuts in income tax shown in Table 10.1 was to increase the incentive to work. Cuts in direct taxation encourage more people to join the labour force or work longer hours, thus boosting labour supply and supply-side growth.

A major initiative of the Labour government (1997-2010) was to vastly extend **tax credits** to poor working families, beginning with the Working Families Tax Credit in 1999. This was then split into two separate tax credits in 2003: the Working Tax Credit is an additional benefit to working individuals or families on low incomes. The Child Tax Credit is paid directly to the main carer of the family, and is designed to tackle child poverty. It is paid regardless of whether people work and families on any income can receive the Child Tax Credit, although high earning households became ineligible from April 2013. The actual amount of child tax credits that a person may receive depends on these factors: the level of their income, the number of children they have, whether the children are receiving Disability Living Allowance and the education status of any children over 16.

Like cuts in income tax during the 1980s, the main aim of tax credits is to **make work pay**. This should reduce the unemployment trap, as the incentive to work is greater. Many earners on low income face very high effective marginal tax rates, as earning more, perhaps through working longer hours will result in the withdrawal of certain benefits (e.g. housing benefit or free school meals) often combined with paying the 20% tax rate on the additional income earned. The Working Tax Credit, therefore, aims to boost the effective take-home income from work for low earners.

The abolition of the 10% starting rate of income tax in 2008 was widely criticised as many households on low income, and young childless single workers in particular, would see their disposable income reduced significantly, reducing the incentive to work. In the face of heavy criticism, the Labour Government expanded their tax credits program to offset this. The Coalition adopted a key Liberal Democrat election pledge to raise the tax free allowance to £10,000 by the end of Parliament in 2015, thereby increasing the incentive to work and lifting millions out of income tax altogether. The tax free allowance had been raised from £6,475 in 2010-11 to £10,000 2014-15. The Conservative government that came to power in 2015 pledged to raise the personal allowance further, to £12,500 by the end of the parliament in 2020.

The Chancellor Alastair Darling announced in the 2009 budget a new top rate of tax at 50% of income above £150,000 which came into effect in April 2010. The Treasury believed it would raise an extra £2.5bn per year. The arguments in favour of the new tax rate include:

- It would help to reduce the size of the large budget deficit.

- It could help to redistribute income.

- The revenue could be used to invest in public services.

- A populist view coming out of the financial crisis and Great Recession was that high earners created the economic problems but were not suffering to the same extent as those on low incomes or those made unemployed, and thus the new top rate was fair, showing that 'we're all in it together'.

Arguments against include:

- Individuals affected may reduce their spending due to a decline in disposable income, with adverse effects on employment and other tax revenues such as VAT.

- It creates a disincentive, reducing income earned and tax taken.

- International labour mobility has increased significantly over the last 20 years, particularly for high earners. Therefore, a 'brain drain' may occur as productive workers migrate to lower tax regimes.

- It may reduce inward foreign direct investment (FDI), and cause companies to move overseas, particularly in financial services where high pay is common.

- It may lead to significant tax avoidance through converting income into capital gains which is taxed at a much lower rate, or moving income to offshore tax havens, or bringing income forward (as was the case in 2009-10 before the rate came into effect).

A Treasury report published in March 2012 revealed that the 50% tax rate was probably yielding only £1bn per year or less, or even a negative yield. In the 2012 budget the Chancellor George Osborne announced a cut in the new top rate to 45%, effective from April 2013.

Evaluation material: Income and substitution effects

If income taxes are cut this will increase the disposable income earned from every hour of work, which may entice the individual to work longer hours. This is known as the **substitution effect**, where the individual substitutes work in place of leisure time. The **income effect** works the other way. A worker might have a target level of post-tax annual income they wish to obtain, and can now achieve this by working fewer hours. Thus, the individual chooses to work less in favour of more leisure time.

Evidence suggests that which effect is greater depends on the individual, but some patterns within groups can be identified. Hours worked by females tend to be quite responsive to income tax cuts, while hours worked by males are almost entirely unresponsive. Both male and female participation rates are very responsive. Overall, direct tax cuts do increase the incentive to work.

● Analysis: Corporation tax

Both the Labour and Coalition governments have followed policies of significantly reducing the corporation tax rate. There are several reasons why such a policy has been pursued. The exchequer have been keen to boost investment which is usually funded from post-tax profits, while continuing to attract large sums of inward FDI from overseas in a world where capital is highly mobile. Furthermore, lower corporation tax rates should encourage greater research and development, enterprise and innovation. All of this should boost long run economic growth. Governments over the last 15 years have been keen to close the unfavourable **productivity gap** between the UK and some of her major competitors such as France and the US (see Chapter 6).

The large company corporation tax rate was lowered from 33% to 30% between 1997 and 1999. In 2000 a 10% starting rate of corporation tax was introduced on profits up to £10,000, with marginal relief applying, meaning companies with profits of between £10,000 and £50,000 paid a rate between the 10% starting rate and the small companies' rate (19% in 2000). The 2007 budget saw the large company corporation tax rate (the rate for profits above £300,000) fall to 28%, and the Coalition Government cut this rate to 21% by April 2014, and the Conservatives cut the rate further to 20% in 2016. Crucially, the Labour government introduced polices which reduced taxation paid on investment. As of 2001 small and medium sized firms were given a 40% capital allowance, and since 2008 most firms can claim a tax allowance on the first £50,000 of spending on plant and machinery.

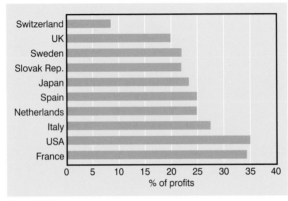

Figure 10.2: International comparison of corporate income tax rates, % of profits (2016)

Source: OECD

Figure 10.2 shows that the UK has a competitive rate of corporation tax relative to her main competitors, but the rate cuts in recent years has been necessary to maintain this position as other countries have also reduced their rates significantly.

Extension material: Capital gains tax

The Labour Government in their early years of office were keen to show that they were 'pro business', and a favourable capital gains tax regime was set up alongside competitive rates of corporation tax. However, there was a perceived lack of fairness within the capital gains tax regime. Many individuals were subject to a 40% capital gains tax while wealthy executives from private equity companies only paid a 10% tax when selling a business, if they had owned it for at least 2 years. In the 2007 budget Chancellor Gordon Brown simplified the system by lowering the main rate from 40% to 18% and ensuring that private equity executives would pay this rate as well by abolishing the previous form of relief. However, many private equity executives still managed to pass off their effective income, known as a 'carry', as capital gains, thus subjecting themselves to an 18% tax rate rather than the much higher rates in the income tax system. As of June 2010, those who pay more than the basic rate of income tax were subject to a 28% capital gains tax.

●● Knowledge and Application: Tax rises

Despite cuts in income and corporation tax, many taxes have risen in recent years, including:

1. Under the Labour and Coalition governments the threshold at which people start paying higher rates of income tax and NICs were not raised in line with inflation, and fell well behind earning growth. For example, between 2010-11 and 2011-12 the higher rate (40%) income tax threshold fell from £37,401 to £35,001. This has dragged more people into higher tax brackets, thus increasing their tax burden. This process is known as **fiscal drag**.

2. The rate of National Insurance paid by most employees, and most employers, has risen considerably since 1997. April 2003 saw a 1% increase in the standard rate of NIC contributions made by both employees and employers. The standard (class 1) employees contribution rate was raised by 1% again in April 2011, to 12%.

3. A number of new, indirect taxes have been introduced since 1992. Examples include the landfill tax, the climate change levy, the insurance premium tax, airport passenger duty and even a sugar tax on soft drinks, announced in the 2016 budget.

4. There have been significant increases in council tax bills since 1997, which is a significant direct tax for most households. Council tax bills in England doubled between 1997 and 2010. Local authorities complained of under-funding from central government while being asked to increase their range of duties, leaving them no choice but to raise council tax bills and collect revenue from other sources such as parking charges. Following the 2010 election Local Government Secretary Eric Pickles put aside a £650m pot to support English councils willing to freeze council tax bills. All English councils took up the offer of support and froze bills in 2011, many continuing to freeze bills through to 2014. Another controversy, however, is that council tax is highly **regressive**. It is paid based on outdated 1991 estimates of property values, and people in houses valued at £320,000 pay the same amount of council tax as those living in houses valued at £2m. Recent council tax rises have raised the tax burden disproportionately for those on low or fixed incomes.

Figure 10.3: Total HMRC receipts, £bn and as a % of GDP (n.b. excluding local taxes)

Source: HMRC

5. As well as the introduction of a number of new taxes, since 1990 a number of indirect taxes have been increased in real terms, including air passenger duty; stamp duty, alcohol and tobacco taxes. In February 2007 air passenger duty was doubled. On the eve of the 2007 budget the Conservatives claimed that Chancellor Brown had raised 99 taxes since he began at the Treasury in 1997. However, Chancellor Osborne cut fuel duty by 1p per litre in his 2011 budget, and planned fuel duty increases were then delayed a further six times thereafter.

6. One of the biggest tax increases in recent years was the increase in VAT in 2011 from 17.5% to 20%, which aimed to reduce the size of the budget deficit. Many criticised the hike in this form of taxation due to its regressive nature. Few however, doubted that this move would raise significant revenue for the government.

Analysis: **Increases in excise duties**

There are several economic justifications for raising excise duties:

● Demand for goods like alcohol, tobacco, and petrol is inelastic. Therefore, a rise in tax will yield significant extra tax revenue for the government.

● Goods subject to excise duties are usually demerit goods which produce negative externalities, and are therefore over-consumed. Indirect taxation helps to correct this **market failure**.

Figure 10.3 shows that the UK tax burden has increased considerably since 1996. This was due to:

● New indirect taxes introduced by Chancellor Brown since 1997 as well as above inflation rises in indirect taxes.

● Higher rate income tax and NIC thresholds rising slower than inflation and earnings.

● Rising employment levels between 1994 and 2007 which boosted income tax and NIC receipts.

● Raising VAT to 20% in January 2011 boosted tax revenue considerably.

Figure 10.3 shows that tax and social security contribution receipts fell considerably due to the recession of 2008-09. The Coalition government, who have committed themselves to reducing the size of the budget deficit, have used a 20/80 rule of thumb; 20% of fiscal consolidation will come from tax rises, 80% will come from spending cuts. Despite the fact that Conservative governments usually favour a smaller state, given the size and persistence of the budget deficit, significant future tax cuts are unlikely.

● ● Knowledge and Application: Government spending

There are two types of government expenditure. **Current expenditure** is public sector spending on goods and services, such as medicines, and other types of recurring expenditure such as public sector salaries. **Capital expenditure** on the other hand, is investment in infrastructure such as motorways, railways, schools and hospitals. Governments have been keen to boost capital spending since 1997, with major projects such as Cross-Rail, and the regeneration of the area surrounding the Olympic Park. The sum of these two types gives Total Managed Expenditure (TME), which reached £772bn in 2016-17.

Figure 10.4 shows that the biggest single area of expenditure is Social Protection, which includes Jobseekers Allowance, Employment and Support Allowance, state pensions and other social security benefits.

Figure 10.4: UK Government spending 2016-17 by area, £bn

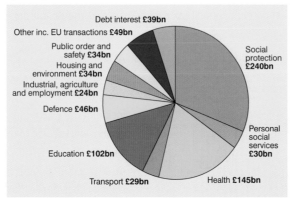

Source: HM Treasury

Figure 10.5: UK government Total Managed Expenditure (TME), £bn

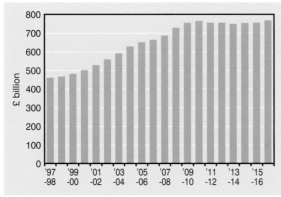

Source: OBR

Figure 10.6: TME as a % of GDP

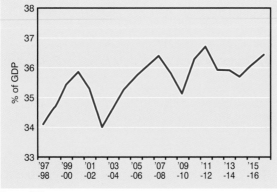

Source: OBR

Analysis of government spending trends

From 2000 onwards Labour increased public spending dramatically. Education, health, transport, housing, crime, and defence all received large increases in real terms expenditure. This spending boosted GDP growth significantly during the period, acting as a **Keynesian stimulus**. The 2002 Comprehensive Spending Review announced an annual average real increase in spending on health of 7.3%, and 5.7% on education, along with big boosts for other departments. Total expenditure on health rose from 6.2% of GDP in 2000 to 8.2% in 2010, finally surpassing the OECD average which the UK lagged behind for decades.

However, the 2008-09 recession caused the budget deficit to increase dramatically, and despite the Coalition government's pledge to protect NHS spending, most government departments have experienced real terms cuts since 2010 as part of their fiscal consolidation strategy. Despite the NHS being 'protected' from spending cuts, an ageing population and the linked pressure on social care have led to increased demand for NHS services, and by

Figure 10.7: UK spending on healthcare as a % of GDP

Source: OECD

2016, a record number of hospitals were reporting crises and a lack of funding.

How beneficial were Chancellor Brown's spending increases?

There are several economic arguments supporting a rise in spending on the NHS. They are:

1. **Rising life expectancy** – The UK has an **ageing population**, who will require more medical care in their old age. Thus, more NHS spending is necessary to provide for their treatment.

2. **Productivity and labour force participation** – Better healthcare should reduce the number of people deemed to be unable to work due to health problems, thereby boosting participation rates and labour supply. Also, a healthier population should be more productive.

3. **Increasing expectations** – Higher standards of living has led to rising consumer expectations of the NHS.

4. **Technological advance** – As new and often expensive drugs and treatments have been discovered, people naturally want them. So new supply has created new demand.

5. **The crisis in the NHS** – By 1997 waiting lists for procedures were long and public spending on health-care as a percentage of GDP was well below most of the UK's European neighbours.

There are several economic arguments supporting a rise in spending on education. They are:

1. **Productivity and competitiveness** – By improving attainment in education the workforce should become more productive, thus increasing supply side growth. As the UK has historically experienced an unfavourable productivity gap to her competitors, improving education is important. Furthermore, in a globalised world, the UK needs a skilled workforce to compete.

2. **Social mobility** – By 1997 many schools in poorer areas were underperforming and dubbed by the term 'sink schools'. By investing heavily in improving schools, particularly in poorer areas and through the academy program, greater equality of opportunity should result, thus improving social mobility, raising aspirations and reducing intergenerational poverty.

3. **Plugging skills gaps** – By the early 2000s there were skills shortages in many sectors which needed addressing.

● Evaluation: Have things improved?

With little doubt there has been a significant improvement in public sector healthcare and education provision since 2000, as well as improvements in other public services. Waiting lists are down, and educational attainment is up, spectacularly in some areas, such as London state schools. However, there is a serious question over how efficient public spending has been. A 2011 report by the ONS revealed that although public service labour input rose by around 15% between 2000 and 2008, labour productivity in the public sector actually fell during this period. In addition a measure of 'value added' public sector output growth lagged well behind the growth in public sector spending during this period, suggesting that higher funding was too often not translated into greater public service provision. A common criticism was that too much funding was used to hire administrative staff and managers, rather than on front line staff and services.

●● Knowledge and Application: Government borrowing

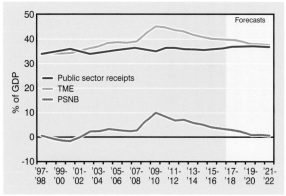

Figure 10.8: Public sector receipts, Total Managed Expenditure (TME) and Public Sector Net Borrowing (PSNB) as a % of GDP

Source: OBR

Public sector net borrowing (**PSNB**) is the sum of government current spending and net capital (investment) spending, minus total tax revenue each financial year. Essentially it is the net amount the government must borrow to finance its spending obligations. Figure 10.8 shows that during Labour's first term the public finances improved considerably. The government ran a budget surplus from 1998-99 to 2000-01, meaning that the PSNB was negative, and the government was able to reduce national debt levels significantly. During Labour's second and third terms however, the public finances worsened considerably. One of the biggest criticisms of Chancellor Brown was that he ran persistent budget deficits from 2001/02 to 2007/08, during a time of strong economic growth. This meant that a **structural budget deficit** was created as shown by the positive PSNB in Figure 10.8 during this period. When the global financial crisis plunged to UK economy into recession in 2008-09, the government was already running a large budget deficit. Falling tax revenue, rising welfare payments and discretionary spending increases caused public sector net borrowing to rise to 10.3% of GDP in 2009-10, leaving the UK with one of the highest budget deficits of all OECD countries. It should also be noted that Figure 10.8 excludes financial sector interventions, particularly the government's bank bail-outs in 2007 and 2008, which cost billions. The government may be able to get this money back when they sell shares in these banks back to the private sector, but the sale of RBS shares back to the private sector, and the sale Northern Rock operations to Virgin Money, both at a lower share price than the government paid for them, cast doubt on this view. Figure 10.8 shows that even with the Coalition and Conservative Governments' fiscal consolidation strategy, the OBR predicts that the budget will not balance until 2022-23 at the earliest. Phillip Hammond, who became Chancellor of the Exchequer in the summer of 2016, formally abandoned his predecessor's plans to balance the budget by 2020. This was mostly due to necessity: growth was forecast to be weaker in the coming years and unemployment slightly higher following the Brexit vote, reducing tax revenues. Also, the government will need to do more to support growth in this period of uncertainty. In the November 2016 Autumn Statement, Mr Hammond announced plans to increase funding for much called for infrastructure projects.

● Analysis: Is the PSNB a problem?

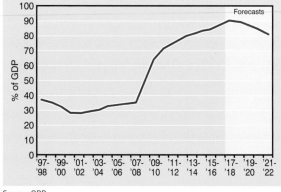

Figure 10.9: UK public sector net debt as % of GDP (excluding financial sector interventions)

Source: OBR

Budget deficits which lead to positive public sector net borrowing can be problematic for the following reasons:

1. **National debt accumulation** – net borrowing year after year leads to growing levels of national (also known as 'public') debt. Note the rising sector debt levels after 2007-08 in Figure 10.9.

2. **Rising interest payments on bonds sold** – The government borrows by issuing paper promises to repay a certain amount borrowed in the future, with interest. This

is known as a **bond**. If the debt burden of a country appears to investors to be unsustainable, they will fear that there is a greater risk that they won't be repaid. Therefore, for the government to continue borrowing they may have to offer higher interest rates to sell bonds, which results in higher borrowing costs, and makes the debt even harder to repay. This is how the debts of Ireland, Greece and Portugal spiralled out of control in 2008-09, resulting in the need for bail-outs from the EU, ECB and IMF.

3. **Future tax rises and spending cut**s – To reduce the rate of public debt accumulation, governments may have to raise taxes or cut spending in the future, which will reduce growth rates. This policy of 'austerity' has been widely implemented in EU countries since 2009.

4. **Crowding-out** – to borrow more, the government may have to raise interest rates on bonds issued, which may cause interest rates across the economy to rise. In turn, this may reduce private sector investment and spending.

5. **Ricardian equivalence** – if the government is running a budget deficit, consumers and firms will anticipate future tax rises and spending cuts. Expecting the resultant lower growth in the future they will save more and spend less. Therefore, the effects of expansionary fiscal policy may be partially offset by the compensating behaviour of households and firms.

Public sector borrowing can be beneficial because:

- It can boost growth at a time when private sector demand is falling, providing a Keynesian fiscal stimulus. Governments around the world collectively ran a fiscal stimulus policy in 2008-09, which helped to prevent a 1930s style depression.

- If borrowing is used to boost capital spending (e.g. new schools, infrastructure), this can lead to productivity growth, thus raising the productive potential of the economy.

● Analysis: Why have the UK government's finances worsened since 2000-01 despite austerity measures designed to improve the budget position?

- Lower tax revenues than expected in the mid 2000s.

- A deliberate large increase in spending on public services during Labour's second and third terms.

- Rising levels of unemployment after 2005 causing a rise in the welfare bill (e.g. more Jobseekers Allowance payments).

- The 2008-09 recession and weak recovery caused falling tax and N.I revenues, as well as a surge in welfare spending. By 2007 10% of the Treasury's tax revenue came from The City.

- Lower company profits, especially due to financial sector losses, reduced tax revenue significantly.

- Government rescues of banks like Northern Rock, Bradford and Bingley and RBS were very costly.

- When the recovery finally got underway in 2013, tax revenues did not increase much owing to low inflation rates, and low rates of earnings growth which reduced the overall 'tax take'.

● ● Knowledge and Application: Labour's fiscal policy framework

The Labour government which took office in 1997 was keen to avoid the persistent budget deficits of the early to mid 1990s, and designed a new fiscal policy framework. The new framework was designed to be *transparent,* and bring *credibility* to fiscal policy, thereby bringing confidence to households and firms. The government set up two specific rules:

1. **The Golden Rule:** The government must only borrow to fund investment, not current spending. Therefore, the government had to **balance the current budget over the economic cycle**. Before the 2008-09 recession the Labour government claimed this rule had been met, but they only achieved this

by changing the start and end dates of the economic cycle in the 2007 budget report, thereby 'moving the goal posts'.

The unexpected severity of the 2008-09 recession led to an enormous increase in the budget deficit and borrowing, as shown in Figure 10.8. The government claimed that the fiscal rules had to be 'flexible' in these exceptional circumstances, but the golden rule was effectively abandoned.

2. **The Sustainable Investment Rule:** Public sector debt would be held at a low and prudent level, not exceeding 40% of GDP. The 2008-09 recession caused repeatedly large budget deficits to be run by the government, causing public debt to soar, as shown in Figure 10.9. In 2014 the Office for Budget Responsibility (OBR) predicted that public sector net debt would peak in 2015-16 at 78.7% of GDP, but by 2017 national debt as a percentage of GDP continued to rise.

Evaluation: Has the government managed the public finances well?

During Labour's first term (1997-2001) they were fiscally prudent, and the public finances improved considerably, with public debt falling as shown in Figure 10.9. After the 2000-01 fiscal year government spending rose considerably. Several taxes were raised and introduced but this was not sufficient to prevent the emergence of repeated budget deficits during a time of strong growth in the mid-2000s. Although the causes of the severe 2008-09 recession were arguably out of the government's control, going into that period running a structural budget deficit did not help, and the government's own fiscal rules had to be abandoned. Having compared favourably before the 2008-09 recession, public debt has risen to levels higher than some other OECD countries, as shown in Figure 10.10, though the Coalition government's policy of 'austerity' improved the relative public debt standing of the UK somewhat.

Figure 10.10: Total gross general government debt 2014, % of GDP

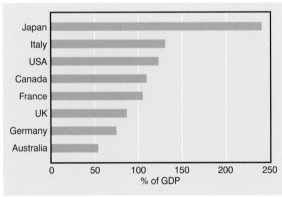

Source: OECD

Figure 10.11: Selected European ten-year government bond yields

Source: Bank of England

Many in the Coalition Government who took office in 2010 were fearful that investors could become alarmed by the rate at which UK public debt was rising, and that they would insist on higher rates of interest on government bonds issued. The Coalition government presented a detailed and strong commitment to budget deficit reduction, through tax rises and departmental spending cuts. Although Labour have criticised the government for cutting 'too far, too fast' and choking off the recovery, the policy has seemed to quell investor fears, as the UK government has been able to borrow at very low rates of interest, as shown in Figure 10.11. In part this has been due to investors fleeing from bond markets in struggling Eurozone economies such as Greece, Portugal, Italy and Spain, with bonds issued by the UK, Germany and the US being seen as relatively 'safe havens'. However, fears of default by the large Southern Eurozone economies of Italy and Spain have subsided, as shown by falling bond yields from mid-2012 in Figure 10.11.

●● Application **and** Analysis: **International comparison of public finances**

Figure 10.12: General government expenditures as a percentage of GDP (2015)

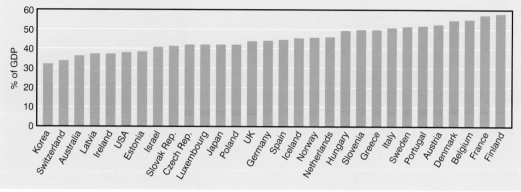

Source: OECD

The UK has traditionally been seen as a middle-to-low ranking country in terms of government spending as a proportion of GDP, embracing free markets more than many of her 'statist' European neighbours. However, Figure 10.12 shows that government spending as a percentage of GDP in the UK has moved close to the Eurozone average and has a 'middle' ranking. This provides further evidence of the Labour government's (1997-2010) more interventionist approach. However, government spending remains considerably lower than countries with a strong social democratic tradition, particularly in Scandinavia. The Coalition's deficit reduction policy was to reverse the trend seen under Labour, as significant public sector job and spending cuts, combined with a robust rise in private sector output and employment is set to continue reducing the public sector's share of GDP. The trend will continue under the new Conservative government.

Figure 10.13: Total tax revenue as a % of GDP (2014)

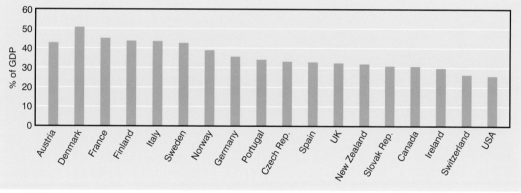

Source: OECD

Figure 10.13 shows that the UK is a middle ranking country in terms of tax revenues. The UK has a higher tax burden than more free market economies such as the United States, but a lower tax burden than more interventionist North European countries. Although the UK does not have high relative tax rates, she does have a high degree of tax compliance, which pushes her up the tax revenue as a proportion of GDP rankings.

●● Knowledge **and** Application: **The impact of the Euro on fiscal policy**

The EU Growth and Stability Pact (GSP) adopted in 1997 stated that countries joining the euro could not run budget deficits exceeding 3% of GDP, and national debt could not rise above 60% of GDP. Although the UK did not join the euro, Labour's fiscal rules followed a similar theme to those adopted by Eurozone countries, which aimed to stop Eurozone governments undermining monetary policy by adopting contrary fiscal policy measures. France and Germany were the first ones to break the GSP. Following this, many Eurozone counties broke the GSP, and on the eve of the global financial crisis in 2007 many Southern

The vote to leave the EU on the 23rd June 2016 has led to growth forecast downgrades

Eurozone countries like Italy, Greece and Portugal had accumulated national debt levels of around 100% of GDP. When the global recession of 2008-09 led to a significant worsening in the public finances in most Eurozone countries the GSP was effectively abandoned, like Labour's fiscal rules. By 2014 Eurozone countries were trying to carve out a new GSP, with greater scrutiny over national budgets by Brussels and harsher penalties for countries who break the rules, to ensure the Eurozone debt crisis is not repeated, but nothing formal was agreed.

Europe, in one form or another, continues to pose a challenge to the state of the UK public finances. Around 40% of the UK's exports go to the Eurozone, which continues to experience weak growth and the underlying causes of the Eurozone crisis remain unresolved, which adds to uncertainty and constrains growth. This reduces UK growth prospects, and with it the chances of an improvement of the UK's fiscal position. The vote to leave the EU on the 23rd June 2016 has led to growth forecast downgrades, which will put further pressure on the public finances, and the budget deficit is set to remain persistently high. If the UK goes into recession in the coming years, the government is in a weak position to deal with such a challenge as the budget deficit, and the level of national debt, are already precariously high.

Chapter 11

The United Kingdom and Europe

This chapter will address the following key questions regarding the UK and Europe in 2017 and beyond:

- What advantages and disadvantages arise from UK membership of the EU?

- What costs and benefits have arisen from EU enlargement?

- What advantages and disadvantages might arise from the UK entering into European Monetary Union (EMU) and replacing sterling with the euro as its currency?

- Given the economic crises in Europe since 2008 and the 'Brexit' decision in 2016, what might the future hold for the EU and the eurozone?

● Knowledge: **The European Union and the Eurozone**

The United Kingdom is still one of the 28 members of the European Union. Table 11.1 shows how the European Union has evolved, from its initial existence as just a free trade area for coal and steel towards deeper and wider economic, social, political and even monetary union.

Table 11.1: EU and eurozone members (as of January 2013)

Year joined EU*	Country	Currency = euro	Year joined EU*	Country	Currency = euro
1952	France	*	2004	Cyprus	*
	Germany	*		Czech Republic	
	Italy	*		Estonia	*
	Belgium	*		Hungary	
	Netherlands	*		Latvia	*
	Luxembourg	*		Lithuania	*
1973	Denmark			Malta	*
	Ireland	*		Poland	
	United Kingdom			Slovakia	*
1981	Greece	*		Slovenia	*
1986	Portugal	*	2007	Bulgaria	
	Spain	*		Romania	
1995	Austria	*	2013	Croatia	
	Finland	*			
	Sweden				

*or equivalent at date of entry

The candidate countries for EU membership are currently Iceland, Montenegro, Serbia, FYR Macedonia and Turkey.

● Analysis: **What are the advantages of membership of the EU?**

The European Union is a **customs union** with free trade between members (freedom of trade in goods and services, freedom of movement of labour and capital) and common external tariffs imposed on imports from outside the EU; every member must set the same tariff (import tax) on imports of agreed goods and services.

The key microeconomic advantages of the **Single European Market (SEM)** are:

- EU members can specialise their production to create and deepen mutual gains from trade.

- The SEM creates European-wide competition, which should drive down costs of production, leading to...
  - Greater efficiency in EU firms
  - Opportunities for successful firms to enjoy economies of scale across Europe-wide markets
  - Lower prices and more choice for EU consumers
  - Greater incentives to invest, leading to dynamic efficiency gains

The key macroeconomic advantages of the SEM are:

- Productivity is raised due to increased efficiency and investment.

- Inflationary pressures are reduced across EU markets.

- Unemployment may fall as real wages rise and free movement of workers eases local labour market problems.

- GDP growth is encouraged.

The UK's Department of Business, Innovation and Skills estimate that EU members trade twice as much with each other as a result of the SEM. Over half of the UK's exports are sold to other EU countries. A European Commission study of the SEM in 2007 found that the SEM raised EU GDP by €233bn, adding 2.2% to GDP, and that 2.75 million jobs were created between the introduction of the single market in 1992 and 2006.

● Analysis: What are the disadvantages of membership of the EU?

Critics of the EU point out the following issues with EU membership:

- Local and domestic unemployment resulting from either work moving overseas or being competed out of existence by lower cost producers from elsewhere in the EU.

- Freedom of movement of labour has created competition in labour markets in countries such as the UK, where net migration has been inward.

- Increased immigration places pressure on public services, housing and infrastructure, particularly in regions where net immigration is particularly high.

- The UK typically contributes approximately £13bn to the EU budget and receives between £4bn and £5bn in return; overall, this makes the budgetary cost of membership to be £8.5 billion.

- A significant portion of the EU budget is spent on the Common Agricultural Policy, which critics argue is inefficient, raises food prices, creates significant food waste and disproportionately benefits major agricultural producing members of the EU.

- As several EU countries have struggled to recover from the credit crisis and the recession which followed, there has been pressure on other EU members to contribute to 'bail-out' funds.

- Trade with other EU members has simply replaced trade which the UK used to conduct with other non-EU economies. **Trade creation** occurs when joining a customs union reduces the price of imported goods. **Trade diversion** occurs when joining a customs union increases the price of imported goods. In the latter case, it could be argued that when the UK joined the EU they were forced to buy more agricultural produce from within Europe, as the newly-imposed common external tariff priced non-EU trading partners such as Australia and New Zealand out of UK markets.

● Knowledge: EU enlargement in practice

The EU has grown from its original six members in 1952 and now forms an economic superpower with a population of over 500 million and a combined GDP of around £11 trillion (larger than the USA and Japan combined).

New members of the EU have to meet three key membership criteria:

● Political: viable institutions which support democracy, human rights and the rule of law.

● Economic: a market economy capable of competing within the SEM.

● Legal: acceptance of EU law (which takes precedence over domestic law) and a willingness to move towards monetary union when appropriate.

● Analysis: What are the implications of an enlarged EU for existing members?

In theory an enlarged EU will enhance the advantages of the SEM given new markets for UK goods in rapidly growing and developing markets. Access to cheaper raw materials and new sources of labour in new member states should also assist economic growth.

However the particular nature of many new members of the EU in recent years (and the future) has raised several concerns:

● New members tend to have lower GDP per capita than the average of existing members, limiting the potential for higher exports and profits for firms in existing states.

● New entrants are likely to be net beneficiaries from the EU budget (particularly if they have relatively large agricultural sectors), putting added pressure on the budget and potentially increasing pressure on existing members to contribute more.

● Workers in new member states may be more likely to emigrate as a result of EU enlargement, increasing immigration into higher income countries.

On this final point, it is worth noting that EU members can restrict immigrants from new members to some extent, and also migrants may be deterred from Western European economies where unemployment remains high after several years of economic decline and stagnation.

Immigration and macroeconomic performance is an important relationship to explore further. Critics of open immigration usually assume that migrants 'steal jobs' or claim benefits unfairly, placing pressure on public finances and public services. However, the eligibility of immigrants for domestic benefits, even when arriving from inside the EU, is not guaranteed and migrant workers can bring several advantages, such as:

● Filling skills gaps in domestic labour markets.

● Higher productivity levels and a stronger work ethic.

● Official economic migrants will pay taxes and make national insurance contributions, boosting the budget position.

● An increased supply of labour can keep wages lower, reducing firms' costs and dampening price inflation pressures.

A study by the Home Office in 2007 suggested that migrant workers to the UK had added £6 billion to UK GDP (creating a net macroeconomic benefit), but at the cost of added strains on public services and housing (thus creating microeconomic costs).

A study published in November 2014 by the Centre for Research and Analysis of Migration[1] at University College, London offers a complex picture of the impact of immigration on the UK. In general, migrants arriving in the UK from other EU members are well-educated (25% of new migrants from Eastern Europe have university degrees, compared with 24% of the UK workforce) and the tax revenue they generate exceeds the benefits they receive. However, there are wider arguments about the role of immigration in reducing wages and productivity (graduate migrants may work in lower paid, lower skilled jobs in the UK than their qualifications suggest) with consequent impacts on total tax revenue.

---

1. http://www.cream-migration.org/files/FiscalEJ.pdf

● ● Analysis and Evaluation: The advantages of European Monetary Union

The creation of the single European currency unit was until relatively recently seen as a major economic success story.

The arguments given in favour of adopting the euro are:

- The elimination of **transaction costs**, or costs of exchanging currencies, when engaging in trade with other eurozone members.

- The removal of **exchange rate uncertainty**, encouraging greater trade and cross-border investment.

- Greater **price transparency**, as the calculations needed to compare prices in different currencies would no longer be necessary.

In effect, a single currency deepens the advantages of a single market to reinforce and extend the gains from trade, both in static terms (at a point in time) and dynamically (over time). However, there are drawbacks and dangers resulting from the adoption of a single currency:

- Menu costs: these are the one-off costs associated with changing prices, financial and commercial equipment, and even the notes and coins themselves.

- Inflation resulting from imperfect information: some economists argue that when a currency changes (for example during decimalisation in the UK in 1971), firms take advantage of consumer uncertainty to increase prices.

- **Loss of economic sovereignty**: this is most obviously the main drawback of joining the eurozone. Since each currency can only have a single interest rate, the responsibility for setting interest rates passes from the country's central bank to the European Central Bank (ECB). In addition, currency depreciation or devaluation against the euro is no longer an option, and thus the country loses both monetary policy and exchange rate policy sovereignty, in other words two of their key policies for controlling the macroeconomy.

Whether a country should adopt the euro or not depends to some extent on the following key factors:

- The exchange rate at which their currency is ultimately converted into euros. If this rate is too high, this will make domestic goods and services uncompetitive against those of other eurozone members. Too low, and imports will be permanently expensive and the standard of living will suffer.

- The importance of policy sovereignty, which is closely linked to:

- The suitability of eurozone-wide policies to the national economy.

The work of the economist Robert Mundell offers an interesting insight into the key characteristics of a single currency area. Mundell's theory of the **Optimal Currency Area** sets out the necessary conditions for successful monetary union. They are:

1. Labour mobility within the currency area.
2. Capital mobility and price and wage flexibility.
3. Economic cycle convergence.
4. Fiscal mechanisms to redistribute funds from higher income to lower income areas.

Taking each in turn, critics of the eurozone argue that a lack of a common language has hindered labour mobility. In addition, prices and wages are more flexible in some economies than others, mainly due to differentials in labour market policies and employee protection. In terms of economic cycles, the recent recession showed that some eurozone economies were able to recover more quickly from the crisis than others. It is interesting to note that the ability of sterling to depreciate against the euro and the dollar during the recession of 2008-09 gave a welcome boost to UK exports, albeit at the cost of higher inflation due to increased import prices. Such a gain – which some economists estimate reduced the severity of the recession by perhaps 1% of UK GDP – would not have been as likely had the UK been a member of the eurozone at this time.

Similarly, in the second half of 2016 the UK economy appeared to benefit from the depreciation in sterling from a recent peak of €1.31/£ in June to €1.10 in October as growth and employment remained stronger than expected.

Figure 11.1: Real GDP growth in the UK and Euro area

Source: HM Treasury

The EU has resisted pressure from some of its supporters to introduce eurozone-wide tax levels. This would remove another lever of policy power from domestic governments, and arguably seriously constrain the only remaining option remaining, that of supply-side policy. Nonetheless, there are redistributive mechanisms in place, most notably Structural Funds (a form of regional policy, targeting EU money into poorer regions for investment in, for example, infrastructure projects) and the European Stability Mechanism (ESM).

Throughout the post-war period the European Union appeared, despite its faults, to be regarded to have a positive impact on the economies of its members, and the other countries around the world which traded with them.

The events of 2016 have dramatically changed the story of 'Europe', and the UK's relationship with it, and the rest of the chapter will examine these key shifts and consider what might happen next.

We will look first at the crises which were already emerging in Europe in the past decade, before moving onto the issue of 'Brexit'.

●● Knowledge and Application: Europe in crisis?

The credit crisis and ensuing recession at the end of the first decade of the 21st century carried major economic implications across Europe, with some economies hit much harder than others. The five most troubled countries were the so-called 'PIIGS': Portugal, Ireland, Italy, Greece and Spain.

The Single European Market and Single European Currency had, between their inception (1992 and 1999 respectively) and 2007, been acclaimed as great successes. However, the pressures on European countries have been very damaging, and include:

● Collapses in the liquidity and profitability of banking sectors, leading to the threat of bank collapses and the need for government bail outs of the financial sector.

● Housing market and stock market crashes, reducing wealth and business and consumer confidence.

● Business bankruptcies and falling profits.

● Rapidly increasing unemployment, particularly for the young.

● Falling tax revenues due to falling incomes, profits and wealth levels.

● Increases in unemployment benefit claimants.

● Resulting pressures on public finances through rising budget deficits and growing national debts.

● Stagnant or negative growth, reducing opportunities for job creation to replace the jobs lost.

The word 'austerity' has re-entered policy speech, both as a microeconomic response to low confidence and the need to make cheaper lifestyle choices, and as an umbrella term for a macroeconomic priority on closing the budget deficit above policies designed to boost growth.

The eurozone area has been forced to address the problem of growing diversity of incomes within its members. Structural Funds have been put under great pressure, both in terms of increased claims on the budget and the questioning of their value for money in the 'richer' economies which, until the recession, were willing and able to make net contributions in the cause of European integration.

In 2010, Europe's finance ministers approved a €750 billion fund called the **European Financial Stability Facility (EFSF)** to provide a rescue package for economies struggling to keep sovereign debt (national debt) under control.

Economies such as Germany and France have advocated conditions on these 'bail outs' to economies such as Greece and Spain. The key problem is that those economies hit hardest by the impact of recession have to make the deepest cuts in spending and increases in taxation to meet budget deficit targets, and these sharply contractionary policies can increase the speed of decline of GDP, leading to ever more severe automatic stabilisation (or fiscal drag) effects.

There are three main sources of funds (the 'troika') for troubled European economies:

● the European Central Bank

● the European Union

● the International Monetary Fund

By November 2012, there were five countries which had requested help from the IMF and the European partners. They were Greece, Cyprus, Spain, Ireland and Portugal.

A key argument put forward by critics of this support was that of **moral hazard**: if economic agents believe they will be helped during a time of difficulty, they may choose to take greater risks with policy-making. In this context, the provision of bail-out funds can be seen as reducing the incentive for governments of engaging in reform to make the necessary cuts in spending or increases in tax to reduce their budget deficits and thus bringing national debt under control.

The summer of 2015 brought a new issue for the economies of the European Union in the form of the humanitarian crisis of over 4 million refugees fleeing war in Syria, with many entering Europe via Turkey.

The pressure on public services, charities and politicians to deal with the influx of vulnerable, displaced people was met in different ways within Europe, from Germany taking over 1 million refugees to the more muted response of the UK's Conservative government, which was already under pressure from its own backbenchers and the electoral threat of the United Kingdom Independence Party to reduce immigration.

Politically, the freedom of movement of people and capital has grown increasingly controversial in recent years, and the economic realities of structural unemployment and widening inequality have brought into question the assumption that free trade (whether global, or within a group of countries such as the EU) is a positive force for progress.

The European Union is open to criticism from opposing directions:

● The EU is too open: freedom of movement disrupts traditional patterns of industry, employment and culture, as native workers and firms face competition (and support) from foreign economic agents

● The EU is too closed: the common external tariff creates 'Fortress Europe' where the economies of its member states are protected from competition in the rest of the world; in particular the Common Agricultural Policy has a detrimental impact on farmers in the developing world

2017 will see major elections in France and Germany, and the politics and economics of migration and national identity will undoubtedly play a significant role in their outcomes.

The next section examines the most important story of 2016, when the first EU country in its history decided to leave the Union. During the financial crisis of 2008-09, there was the overriding fear of 'Grexit': Greece being forced out of the Eurozone. This was avoided, but now 'Brexit' looms as an existential threat to the European Union.

Evaluation: 'Brexit means Brexit'?

In June 2016, the people of the UK voted by a majority of 17.4 million to 16.1 million to leave the European Union. This was a shock result: opinion polls had shown a small majority in favour of continued membership, and in the days after the result the impact was seen in volatile financial markets. The main medium-term impact has been a dramatic depreciation in the value of sterling against the euro, and against other major currencies such as the US dollar.

The new Prime Minister, Theresa May, has repeatedly stated that 'Brexit means Brexit', and that in early 2017 the government will invoke Article 50, the process set out in the Lisbon Treaty of 2009, and two years later the UK will cease to be a member of the EU.

How this affects the UK economy is incredibly difficult to predict, and will depend on the trade deals the government can negotiate with the EU and other economies around the world. What is certain is that a failure to reach a deal will lead to UK exports into the EU being subject to the Common External Tariff (along with all other non-EU countries selling into the EU market) and a loss of freedom of movement of UK workers into the EU labour market.

It could be the case that the UK retains some of the features of EU membership, a phenomenon known as 'Soft Brexit' in contrast to a full separation, coined as 'Hard Brexit' by some commentators.

The different options regarding the 'softness' of Brexit show the complex structure of the European Union.

Soft Brexit: one option is the UK retains access to the Single European Market and its four freedoms (freedom of trade in both goods and services, freedom of movement of both labour and capital) perhaps in return for a per-capita 'fee' to replace the GDP-weighted contribution to the EU budget, and acceptance of EU regulations and laws.

This 'Norway model' would see the UK become a member of the European Economic Area (EEA) which comprises the EU economies and Norway, Liechtenstein and Iceland.

In reality, this level of integration between the UK and EU may prove politically unacceptable: the EU referendum did not state what the relationship should look like if the country voted 'Leave' but free movement of labour and the fee for access would be controversial to some.

European Free Trade Association: members of the EFTA such as Switzerland enjoy tariff-free trade in goods with EU states, but protectionism is in place for most services, and crucially for the banking industry. The financial contribution required would be lower than for full access, and Switzerland's experience has been that the successful negotiation of trade deals has depended on issues such as freedom of movement of people.

EU Trade Deal: the UK and EU will have two years to negotiate bilateral trade agreements which might be general (e.g. all industrial goods) or specific (e.g. for a specific good or service); the outcome of such a deal will depend on the attitude of EU exporters to the potential loss or increased cost of trade with the UK market, and the UK's dependence on the EU as both a market for its output and a source of raw materials. Trade barriers such as tariffs (including the Common External Tariff system) and quotas increase the costs of cross-border trade but negotiations to reduce them are usually very lengthy and measured in years, if not decades.

World Trade Organisation (WTO) rules: this is the most 'Hard' of Brexit possibilities and is the default if no agreement is reached within the two year period after Article 50 is invoked: the UK will in this case have to make no financial contribution to the EU and have no obligation to offer free movement to any non-UK worker or citizen. In this case, arrangements for EU and non-EU workers in the UK will become the same, and subject to the same visa arrangements.

Free Trade: a final, if unlikely, option is the UK opens its economy to free trade and imposes no tariffs, quotas or regulation in imports. Even if this were the ultimate goal of free-market economists, a prudent approach would be via the WTO option and trade negotiations with as many countries and trading blocs as possible towards achieving free trade.

The relationship the UK has with its trading partners is therefore uncertain, but key issues which will be important to consider in years ahead are:

- How important is the UK market to EU exporters?

- How important is the EU market to UK exporters? For both of these points, this will depend on relative growth rates in the UK and EU27, and also developments in the wider world economy, specifically patterns of demand in both developed economies and emerging markets

- Impacts on foreign direct investment (FDI): unless the UK can negotiate otherwise, its exports to EU states will be subject to the common external tariff and this has raised concerns that this will make the UK a less attractive place for multinational companies to locate. Since the referendum result, a number of MNCs have announced new or continued investment in the UK, for example Nissan's decision to keep their plant in Sunderland

- Government macroeconomic policy: tariff-free trade is important to firms, but they can also be influenced in location decisions by infrastructure investment, subsidies for research and development, and training and technological innovation; the UK government has given 'assurances' (the nature of which were unspecified and thus unclear in terms of cost) to firms such as Nissan that they are seeking free trade with the EU and the Autumn Statement in 2016 outlined business-friendly policies. Corporation tax rates will be decreased from 20% to 19% in 2017 and 17% from 2020 to keep the UK attractive as a place to base operations and employ workers; it is also possible that employee rights will be reduced post-Brexit

- Impacts on the financial sector: the loss of UK banking activity and jobs to alternative European centres such as Paris or Frankfurt is likely unless an agreement can be made on 'passporting', the agreement which currently allows UK financial institutions to process euro payments in London

- Impacts on the UK labour market and public services: much of the anti-immigrant rhetoric in the referendum campaign focused on how migrant labour takes jobs from British workers and puts strain on public services such as the NHS and public transport; however, this needs to be balanced by the contribution foreign workers make to the economy with their skills and effort

- Trade deals: the UK is a large and dynamic economy and we will see in the years ahead to what extent it can leverage this status in its negotiations with the EU and non-EU countries and blocs

The Chancellor, Phillip Hammond, released data in the Autumn Statement of November 2016 that the decision to leave the EU is estimated to cost the UK's public finances £60bn by 2020, effectively ending the promise by his predecessor to balance the budget by 2020.

The future is uncertain, arguably more uncertain than at any other time in recent years, and the impact of Brexit will depend on too many factors, some political rather than economic, for a prediction to be possible or helpful. A wider debate to consider is how a post-EU economy such as the UK considers not just the level of GDP and employment and tax receipts, but also the distribution of income, benefits and wealth. The free market, free trade Brexit model which looks likely may create greater overall prosperity, but if the experience of households is longer working hours and lower real pay, alongside declining or privatised public services, it is hard to imagine a future where the quality of life of the average Briton is anything but degraded.

Questions

1. Explain the benefits of EU membership to a candidate country such as Montenegro.

2. What factors might determine the overall impact of membership of the EU to countries such as Sweden, Belgium and Bulgaria?

3. Evaluate the impact of Brexit on the economic performance of (i) the UK, (ii) the remaining members of the EU.

Chapter 12

The UK in the World Economy

This chapter examines the UK's position in the global economy, as well as the challenges and opportunities the UK economy is likely to face in the coming decades. The result of the referendum on the UK's membership of the EU in 2016 brings these issues into sharp focus.

● Knowledge: The UK and globalisation

Globalisation is such a multi-faceted issue that it is hard to define precisely. Globalisation can be taken to mean the increasingly free flows of goods, services, capital, people, information and cultures around the world. Advocates of globalisation and free trade believe that countries will specialise in their area of **comparative advantage**. This is where one country can produce a good or service at a lower opportunity cost than another. Put simply, the theory implies that if each country specialises in producing the good or service they are relatively best at, resources will be allocated more efficiently, total global output should rise, and overall economic welfare will be improved. The NICE decade between 1997 and 2007 was a period of rapid globalisation. However, the 2008 sub-prime mortgage crisis in the US sent shockwaves through highly integrated financial markets, and caused a global economic recession. Similarly, problems in Greece, Ireland and Portugal had negative effects across the Eurozone and beyond in 2011, showing that globalisation increases an economy's vulnerability to external shocks. Anti-globalisation movements have been growing in voice across Europe and North America. The growing popularity of the National Front party in France, and the popularity of Donald Trump's anti-free trade rhetoric in the run up to the November 2016 Presidential Election are just two examples. In the UK, many voters who supported Brexit cited concerns over the level of immigration, and the rapid pace of change, as reasons for wanting to leave the EU.

Figure 12.1: Merchandise Trade (% of GDP), selected countries

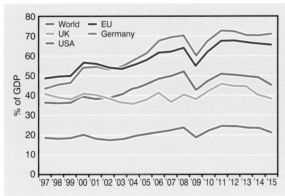

Source: WTO

Figure 12.2: Manufacturing and Financial Services as a % of GDP

Source: ONS data from HM-Treasury budget 2012

● Analysis: How has globalisation affected the UK economy?

As shown in Figure 12.1, growth in global trade tends to rise more rapidly than world GDP growth, implying that imports and exports as a percentage of GDP have been rising in most countries, due to the increasingly free movement of goods and services. Figure 12.1 shows that between 1997 and 2007 global merchandise trade grew from around 38% of global GDP to over 50%. Global trade then fell sharply during the 2008-09 global recession, before stabilising at pre-crisis levels in from 2011.

The UK economy has seen growing import and export volumes over the last two decades (see Chapter 5 for more detail). For the UK, the value of imports and exports of goods and services was close to 30% of GDP in 2016.

Figure 5.1 in Chapter 5 highlights the UK's move to specialise in the production of services, in which it is a large net exporter, at the expense of manufactured goods, in which the UK is now an enormous net importer. Over the past two decades, Newly Industrialised Countries (NICs) such as China and others in the Asian Pacific Rim have become able to produce manufactured goods at a much lower cost than producers in the UK and other Most Developed Countries (MDCs). At the same time the UK has a clear comparative advantage in the production of services due to the use of English as the international business language, a long standing reputation for excellence in professional services such as accounting, law and finance, and the existence of the City of London as the world's leading financial centre.

Figure 12.3: Gross Value Added attributable to manufacturing in the G7 economies and China (% nominal GVA, 1947-2012), black triangles mark historical UK data

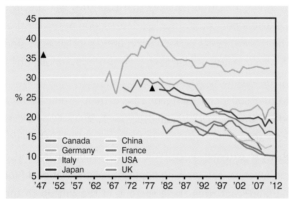

Source: World Bank

Figure 12.4: UK GDP and financial services output growth

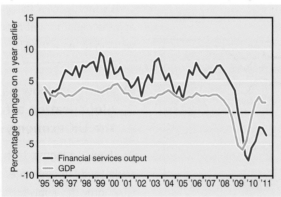

Source: Bank of England

Figure 12.5: Financial and insurance output in the G7 economies (% of nominal GVA)

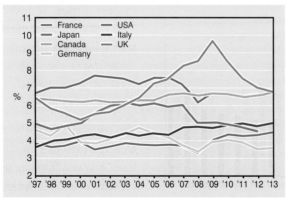

Source: OECD

Figure 12.2 shows that the manufacturing sector has shrunk considerably as a proportion of the UK output since 1997, while financial services have grown in importance. According to the ONS business services and finance accounted for 29.3% of GDP in 2012, with manufacturing accounting for just 10.3% of GDP, and just 8% of jobs in 2014. Since the 1980s the UK's relatively more relaxed attitude towards free markets has led to governments doing less to support manufacturing in the face of new competition from East Asia than many of her competitors such as France and Germany, and significant deindustrialisation occurred. The manufacturing sector's share of UK GDP fell to levels significantly lower than France and Germany, as shown in Figure 12.3. Areas of Southern Scotland, South Wales and Northern England have been particularly affected by industrial decline. Some of these areas remain blighted by high rates of unemployment and welfare dependency.

While manufacturing has declined as a share of GDP, Figure 12.4 shows that in the decade leading up to the 2008 financial crisis, GDP growth averaged 3% per annum while financial services output averaged around 6%, increasing the sector's share of GDP considerably.

Figure 12.5 shows that financial services' share of UK GVA has risen considerably between 2000 and 2008 to levels far higher than in similar-sized European economies such as France, Germany and Italy.

There are problems associated with being dependent on services and financial services in particular. Firstly services are more difficult to export than goods due to language barriers and regulation. The European Union, the destination for over 45% of UK exports, has very effectively removed barriers to trade in goods but has been much less successful in removing barriers to trade in services. Exporting services outside of the EU is even more difficult. As shown in Figure 5.1, the trade in services surplus does not match the trade in goods deficit, leading to a persistent overall trade deficit. The second problem is that there are risks associated with being dependent on finance and banking. Unlike other sectors, if banks get into trouble and go bust there are much wider implications for the economy. Households and firms will lose their savings; other banks will become much less willing to lend and business and consumer confidence will plummet. In 2007-08 some of the UK's biggest banks such as RBS and HBOS faced bankruptcy. The Labour government decided that the consequences of not bailing out these banking giants would be too great to risk, and spent billions of pounds saving them. Given that the share prices of the rescued banks have remained well below their level at the time of the bail-outs, it looks likely the bail-outs will be costly for UK taxpayers.

Globalisation has also had an impact on wage growth across different sectors, and has been blamed for rising wage inequality. Demand for low-skilled manufacturing products has declined, and the UK has a comparative disadvantage in this area. Less demand for basic manufactures means less demand for low-skilled manufacturing workers, thus putting downward pressure on the wages of these workers. At the same time greater demand for UK professional services, the UK's areas of comparative advantage, has increased demand for workers in sectors such as financial and legal services, putting upward pressure on wages in these already well paid jobs. Therefore, greater trade flows and specialisation partly explains widening inequality in original income over much of the past 25 years (see Chapter 4), but the increasingly free flow of workers has also played a role. High net immigration, particularly since the UK opened her borders to the 10 new EU member states in 2004 has increased the supply of relatively unskilled labour in the UK. Some argue this has put downward pressure on wages in unskilled jobs. Some estimates suggest that between 2004 and 2006 as many as 600,000 people came from Eastern Europe to the UK, most of them from Poland. The Conservatives made an election pledge in 2010 to reduce net immigration to below 100,000 per year, but this target was never likely to be met and net immigration reached 336,000 in 2015.

Figure 12.6: Long-Term International Migration, UK, 1970 to 2015 (annual totals)

Source:ONS

The effect of immigration on wages and employment are hotly contested. Most research shows that there is no tangible effect on unemployment rates, as migrant workers add to demand for goods and services and therefore demand for labour, as well as supplying labour. The evidence on the effect of wages, however, suggests that immigration contributes to higher real wages for the higher earners, and lower wages for unskilled labour. Crucially, however, research shows that this effect is very small. Nonetheless, concerns over the impact of unrestricted immigration from other EU countries on wages, employment opportunities, and community cohesion, was a major reason why the UK public voted to leave the EU on 23rd June 2016. The 'Leave' campaign's argument that the UK could only fully control her borders if she left the EU proved a popular argument with voters.

Although 'taking back control' of the UK's borders was a popular notion during the referendum campaign, as was the move to try to finally achieve the 100,000 net migration target, some pointed to the fact that immigration to the UK from **non-EU** countries has been persistently higher than immigration from EU countries. Non-EU immigration to the UK consistently exceeded 100,000 on its own in the run up to the Brexit vote, as shown in Figure 12.7, and the UK government does have 'control' over non-EU migration. It should be noted, however, that around half of non-EU migrants come to the UK to study, which effectively adds to export revenue, and does not add to competition in the jobs market.

Figure 12.7: Net Long-Term International Migration by citizenship, UK, 1975 to 2015

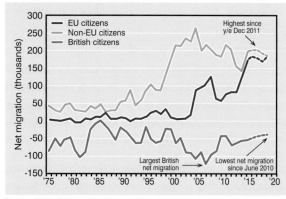

Source: ONS

Figure 12.8: Top 20 countries by Gross Domestic Product (GDP) 2016, $m

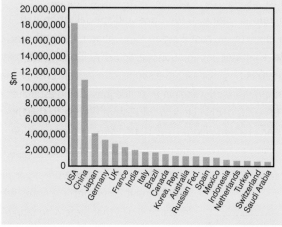

Source: World Bank

● Knowledge: The UK's relative economic standing

Much has been made in recent years of the rise of East Asia, with economies such as China experiencing rapid economic growth, and the relative decline of the West. There is no doubt that the balance of economic power is changing dramatically, especially as many Eurozone economies are still struggling to recover from the 2008-09 recession and the subsequent Eurozone debt crisis. However, it is important to note that the UK, along with Japan, North America and other West European economies still have a dispropor-tionate share of global income.

Figure 12.8 shows that the UK has the fifth largest economy in the world. The UK's share of world GDP is roughly 4%, despite having less than 1% of world population.

Table 12.1 shows that as an open economy, the UK ranks highly in the world share of imports and exports of goods and services. The fact that the UK is the world's second largest exporter of commercial services clearly demonstrates her comparative advantage in this area. In contrast, the UK is only the eleventh largest exporter of goods.

The UK's relative economic position is forecast to decline in the years to come. Brazilian GDP eclipsed that of the UK in 2011, albeit temporarily, and India, Russia and Mexico are all forecast to have bigger economies than the UK by 2026.

Table 12.1: Merchandise and commercial services trade: leading exporters and importers, 2011, by rank and % of world total (merchandise trade, left-hand side; services, right-hand side)

Rank	Goods exporters	Share (%)	Goods importers	Share (%)	Rank	Service exporters	Share (%)	Service importers	Share (%)
1	China	10.4	USA	12.3	1	USA	13.9	USA	10.1
2	USA	8.1	China	9.5	2	UK	6.6	Germany	7.3
3	Germany	8.1	Germany	6.8	3	Germany	6.1	China	6.1
4	Japan	4.5	Japan	4.6	4	China	4.4	UK	4.4
5	Netherlands	3.6	France	3.9	5	France	3.9	Japan	4.3
6	France	3.3	UK	3.5	6	India	3.6	France	3.6
7	Rep. of Korea	3.0	Netherlands	3.2	7	Japan	3.4	India	3.4
8	Italy	2.9	Italy	3.0	8	Spain	3.4	Netherlands	3.1
9	Russia	2.9	Rep. of Korea	2.9	9	Netherlands	3.1	Italy	3.0
10	Belgium	2.6	Hong Kong	2.8	10	Singapore	3.0	Ireland	2.9
11	UK	2.6	Canada	2.5	11	Hong Kong	2.9	Singapore	2.9
12	Hong Kong	2.5	Belgium	2.5	12	Ireland	2.6	Canada	2.6
13	Canada	2.5	India	2.5	13	Italy	2.6	Rep. of Korea	2.5
14	Singapore	2.2	Singapore	2.0	14	Switzerland	2.3	Spain	2.4
15	Saudi Arabia	2.0	Spain	2.0	15	Rep. of Korea	2.3	Russia	2.3

Source: WTO

Extension material: Income convergence or divergence?

At the end of the Second World War, GDP per person in Western Europe was around half that of the US, and Japan's GDP per person was around one sixth. By 1990, income per person was roughly the same in these economies. Clearly **convergence** occurred between developed countries. Income per person in Newly-Industrialised Countries (NICs) is rapidly catching up with levels in MDCs such as the UK, and some of the original Asian Tiger economies such as Hong Kong, Singapore and South Korea now have income levels comparable to, or even higher than, most MDCs in the West. Global trade has grown enormously since 1945. The **Heckscher-Ohlin theory** states that with trade, capital intensive economies will tend to produce capital intensive goods as they can do so more efficiently than labour intensive economies, which will produce labour intensive products. Samuelson's **Factor Price Equalisation theory** states that if the cost of one factor of production (e.g. workers) is lower than another factor of production (e.g. capital) before trade takes place, it will rise relative to the other once trade takes place. Evidence from the US and China support this theory. The US has an abundance of capital compared to China, which has a relative abundance of labour. Since 1980, trade between the two countries has grown enormously. In China, wages have grown significantly. For example, unit labour costs in China rose by 9% in 2011, thus raising the cost of relatively abundant labour compared to relatively scarce capital. In the US, median real wage growth has stagnated since the late 1970s, thus lowering the cost of relatively scarce labour compared to the more abundant capital. The UK's experience has been very similar to that of the US, although median real income growth has been slightly higher. Although average income per person in China is around one tenth of average income in the UK, a process of **convergence** is clearly taking place. As wages in China rise, more capital is being used in the production process. In the US, as wage costs have been falling relative to the cost of capital, the US has experienced a 're-shoring' of manufacturing, as manufacturing domestically becomes more cost-effective than importing from China. There is now some evidence that 're-shoring' of manufacturing has begun in the UK as well. However, this process has also occurred due to rising transport costs and technological advances from fracking reducing energy costs in US production plants. Despite some signs of convergence income per capita in many of the Least Developed Countries (LDCs) such as Congo and Myanmar has fallen behind incomes in MDCs, showing a **divergence** between the top and the bottom of the global income distribution. Several economic models, including the **Solow Growth model**, suggest that a certain amount of capital must be accumulated before an economy can '**take off**', and achieve self-sustaining economic growth. To accumulate capital, economies must have reasonably high savings ratios, or bring in capital from overseas, through trade or access to finance from institutions such as the World Bank. Many economies in Sub-Saharan Africa are unable to accumulate sufficient capital. Poverty leads to low savings rates, primary product dependency leaves countries vulnerable to a worsening in the terms of trade, which means they can import less in exchange for their exports. In addition, some economists believe that LDCs must reach a certain 'social capacity' before they can take-off, through reducing problems such as corruption and health issues to a critical level that allows for self-sustaining growth to take place.

Analysis: How would 'rebalancing' help the UK economy?

Switching from consumption and imports, to investment and exports

Since the financial crisis started in 2008, there has been a consensus amongst policymakers and economists that the UK economy has become too dependent on consumption (fuelled by excessive household borrowing) and imports. The Conservatives in particular also believe that the UK economy has become too dependent on government spending, funded by excessive public sector borrowing. The Bank of England and the Coalition government both called for a 'rebalancing' of the economy away from consumption and imports, towards investment and exports. This should help to bring more balanced and sustainable growth. A consensus has also emerged that the UK economy has become too dependent on services, and the manufacturing base of the economy has shrunk too much. Therefore many believe that boosting the manufacturing sector's share of the economy should be part of the rebalancing process.

Despite the consensus that rebalancing would be beneficial, there have been few specific policy initiatives designed to help the rebalancing of the UK economy. After a 24% depreciation in 2008, the pound settled at a lower value than during the NICE decade (1997-2007), and fell by over 10% in June 2016 following the Brexit vote. This should help to improve net exports, but the weaker pound is not the result of deliberate government policy. One government initiative to boost 'green' investment is the founding of the **UK Green Investment Bank** in 2012. The plc aims to attract private funds to finance the private sector's investments related to environmental improvements. The **Funding for Lending Scheme** (**FLS**) set up jointly by the Treasury and the Bank of England in 2012 aims to boost investment by enabling banks to borrow at lower rates on the condition that they lend more to businesses and consumers. One criticism of quantitative easing (QE) is that much of the cash injection has been stuck in the financial system, with banks remaining unwilling to lend, and many small businesses complain about the lack of access to credit, which impedes investment. The FLS aims to address this, as does the **Term Funding Scheme** introduced in August 2016, by increasing the amount of loans given to businesses, thus increasing investment.

Figure 12.9: OBR forecast change in shares of GDP 2011-16

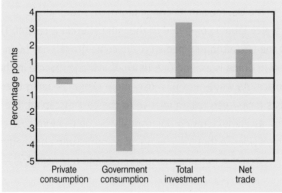

Source: OBR

Figure 12.9 shows that the government expected the share of GDP accounted for by consumption and government spending to shrink, the latter by some 4.5%, and the contribution of investment and net trade to grow as a share of GDP between 2011 and 2016. The fall in government consumption's share of GDP is mostly due to the spending cuts in an attempt to reduce the size of the budget deficit.

Despite some glimmers of hope, by 2016 there was little evidence to suggest that significant rebalancing had taken place, either in terms of the components of GDP in Figure 12.9, or between the manufacturing and service sectors. According to the ONS, since the Coalition took office in the second quarter of 2010, manufacturing accounted for 10.7% of GDP, and business services and finance accounted for 28.8%. By 2013, manufacturing's share of the economy had shrunk to 10% of GDP, with manufacturing output 8.9% below its pre-crisis peak, while business services and finance output had grown to 32% of GDP. Exports of goods and services have increased since the depths of the 2008-09 recession, but so have imports, and there has been no significant improvement in the trade balance, and the trade in goods deficit is bigger than ever (see Chapter 5). Total managed expenditure (TME) by government was at a similar level in 2016-17 as a proportion of GDP (around 36%) than on the eve of the financial crisis in 2007-08 (see Figure 10.6), while private sector investment's share of GDP is lower than pre-crisis levels, at 15.1% of GDP in 2013 compared to 17.1% in 2008. The uncertainty created by the Brexit vote is widely predicted to cause many firms to delay investment plans until they know what the UK's future trading arrangements will be, and what sort of access they will have to the EU single market. If the shares of GDP in the UK economy do rebalance, it is likely to take some time.

● Analysis: **What can the UK do to boost net exports?**

Many countries in the Eurozone have been gripped by an ongoing debt crisis and uncertainty over the future of the currency union since the world economy went into recession in 2009. As a result growth in Eurozone economies remains very weak, and many euro area economies have slipped back into recession since 2009. Around 40% of the UK's exports go to Eurozone countries. Figures 12.10 and 12.11 show that weak GDP growth in the Eurozone has caused consumers to purchase fewer imports, thus causing the Eurozone import growth to stagnate. This means there is little potential for a significant rise in demand for

Figure 12.10: Eurozone quarterly GDP growth rates (%QoQ)

Source: OECD

Figure 12.11: Eurozone quarterly imports of goods ($bn)

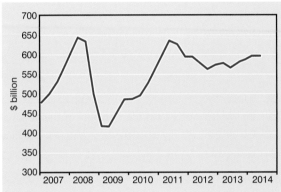

Source: OECD

Figure 12.12: Value of UK goods and services exported to EU and non-EU countries (£bn)

Source: Bank of England

UK exports from Eurozone members, reducing the likelihood of an export-led recovery and a 'rebalancing' of the economy towards exports.

Faster growing developing economies, on the other hand, provide a significant opportunity for export growth, and since 2010 governments have been keen to boost trade relations with these countries. On taking office in 2010 the Prime Minister David Cameron visited several of these countries on trade missions, including Brazil, China and the UAE. Germany has been very successful at growing exports, usually of hi-tech manufactures and capital goods, to the fast growing developing economies, the BRICs in particular. German exports to China for example more than doubled between January 2007 and January 2012. The UK however, has so far been less successful at 're-orienting' trade towards these emerging markets, which is disappointing, but there is a clear opportunity for growth in this area. As well as trade deals, the stabilisation of the pound at below pre-financial crisis levels should help to make UK exports more competitive.

Despite not being as successful at re-orienting trade towards emerging markets compared to other advanced European economies, UK exports to both India and China rose by around 55% in the 5 year period after January 2007, and Figure 12.12 shows that by 2009, for the first time in decades, UK exports of goods and services to non-EU countries exceeded exports to EU countries, and non-EU countries accounted for 56% of all UK exports in 2016. This is partly due to the fragile state of the EU economy, but it can partly be explained by rising exports to emerging markets. Perhaps most importantly, Brexit provides an opportunity for the UK to cut ties with the EU and instead strike trade deals with faster growing economies such as India, China, and Australia, providing a possible engine for export growth. Whether this occurs or not depends on whether the UK undertakes a 'hard' or 'soft' departure from the EU.

Outlook for the UK economy

The medium term outlook for the UK economy is highly uncertain. Since the 2008-09 recession growth forecasts have proved highly inaccurate, frequently over-predicting growth between 2009 and 2012, but the pace of GDP and employment growth from 2013 to 15 took many by surprise when the recovery finally arrived in earnest. There are however, many who doubt the sustainability of growth. Firstly, many economists believe that the recovery so far has been based on increases in consumption due to a falling savings ratio and rapid house price growth, centred in London and the South-East. It is not the balanced, broad-based growth that policy-makers had hoped for. Secondly, despite a rapid increase in employment in 2013-16, many question how 'inclusive' the recovery has been, as OBR data shows that nominal wage growth lagged behind inflation from 2010 until the second half of 2014 meaning real total pay fell, causing a substantial squeeze on living standards. In addition, most of the jobs created since the Great Recession are part-time of temporary jobs. There also remains the ever-present downside risk to UK economic growth from stagnation in the Eurozone and the threat of a prolonged period of Japanese-style deflationary stagnation since exists. This would impact negatively on the UK economy through lower exports, reduced business and consumer confidence, and a possible banking crisis in the event of sovereign credit defaults. In addition, growth in emerging markets such as Brazil and China has weakened, making a rebalancing of growth more difficult than ever. Finally, with the budget deficit and borrowing remaining stubbornly high, continued austerity measures will put downward pressure on growth. However, there are reasons for optimism. The educational attainment of the workforce is higher than ever, and unemployment is only expected to rise to 5.6% in 2017 as a result of the slowdown caused by the Brexit vote. In the longer term however, the performance of the UK economy is likely to depend on whether a return of productivity growth can be achieved, combined with a rebalancing of the economy away from consumption and imports towards investment and exports.

'Hard' vs. 'Soft' Brexit

Of vital importance to the UK's future macroeconomic performance is the outcome of the negotiations to leave the EU. There seem to be two broad schools of thought on what the best outcome for leaving the EU would be. Those who favour a 'soft' Brexit would like the UK to remain part of the Single European Market (SEM), or at least have access to the EU single market in a free trade arrangement. This would mean the UK retains its free trade arrangement with the world's biggest economic area. This model for Brexit would mean that businesses have broadly the same arrangements they have now, which would boost confidence. Those who favour a 'hard' Brexit, such as the group *Economists for Brexit*, say that this would mean that the UK would have to comply with EU regulations, without a say in making them, and crucially, staying part of the SEM means that you have to accept free movement of people, as Norway and Switzerland do, something that is likely to be politically impossible, despite the economic benefits that immigration brings. Those who favour a 'hard' Brexit point to the fact that India, China, Australia and other countries have been quick to ask the UK for a trade deal, and Donald Trump, US President-Elect as of November 2016, said that the UK would be the 'first in the queue' when it came to negotiating a trade deal with the US. In the event of a 'hard' Brexit, the UK would be able to reduce immigration from the EU, but trading arrangements would be far more uncertain, as in the worst scenario the UK would have to adopt WTO rules, and exports to the EU would face the same tariff as any other country that does not have a trade deal with the EU. There would of course be benefits to no longer contributing to the EU budget, and curbing immigration would be popular, but whether the UK can continue to be an attractive destination for FDI, and can continue to trade openly with her European neighbours, would remain to be seen. A 'third way' could be a bespoke, sector-by-sector deal with the EU, with some restrictions of EU immigration. The UK is very keen to retain open access to the EU in the Financial Services industry, while German car manufacturers are keen to have open access to the lucrative UK market. This pragmatic approach, which satisfies mutual interests, could be middle ground, but on the eve of the negotiations pragmatism and goodwill are in relatively short supply, with many in the EU taking a hard line, saying the UK must pay an economic price in order to prevent other countries from wanting to leave the union.

Extension Question

To what extent will a rise in protectionism and a movement away from globalisation impact on economic performance in the UK?